W9-CRK-894

# DRAMATIC AND LATER POEMS

MACMILLAN AND CO., Limited
LONDON · BOMBAY · CALCUTTA · MADRAS
MELBOURNE

THE MACMILLAN COMPANY
NEW YORK · BOSTON · CHICAGO
DALLAS · SAN FRANCISCO

THE MACMILLAN CO. OF CANADA, Ltd.
TORONTO

College of the Pacific
Stockton, Calif.

# POEMS

BY

# MATTHEW ARNOLD

DRAMATIC AND LATER POEMS

New York
THE MACMILLAN COMPANY
1924

PR
4020
A4
1924

PRINTED IN GREAT BRITAIN

# CONTENTS.

## DRAMATIC POEMS.

## LATER POEMS.

# DRAMATIC POEMS

# MEROPE

## A TRAGEDY

# STORY OF THE DRAMA.

APOLLODORUS says:—"Cresphontes had not reigned long in Messenia when he was murdered together with two of his sons. And Polyphontes reigned in his stead, he, too, being of the family of Hercules; and he had for his wife, against her will, Merope, the widow of the murdered king. But Merope had borne to Cresphontes a third son, called Æpytus; him she gave to her own father to bring up. He, when he came to man's estate, returned secretly to Messenia, and slew Polyphontes and the other murderers of his father."

Hyginus says:—"Merope sent away and concealed her infant son. Polyphontes sought for him everywhere in vain. He, when he grew up, laid a plan to avenge the murder of his father and brothers. In pursuance of this plan he came to king Polyphontes and reported the death of the son of Cresphontes and Merope. The king ordered him to be hospitably entertained, intending to inquire further of him. He, being very tired, went to sleep, and an old man, who was the channel through whom the mother and son used to communicate, arrives at this moment in tears, bringing word to Merope that her son had disappeared from his protector's house, and was slain. Merope, believing that the sleeping stranger is the murderer of her son, comes into the guest-chamber with an axe, not knowing that he whom she would slay was her son; the old man recognised him, and withheld Merope from slaying him. The king, Polyphontes, rejoicing

at the supposed death of Æpytus, celebrated a sacrifice; his
guest, pretending to strike the sacrificial victim, slew the king,
and so got back his father's kingdom."

The events on which the action of the drama turns belong
to the period of transition from the heroic and fabulous to the
human and historic age of Greece. The doings of the hero
Hercules, the ancestor of the Messenian Æpytus, belong to
fable; but the invasion of Peloponnesus by the Dorians under
chiefs claiming to be descended from Hercules, and their settle-
ment in Argos, Lacedæmon, and Messenia, belong to history.
Æpytus is descended on the father's side from Hercules, Perseus,
and the kings of Argos; on the mother's side from Pelasgus, and
the aboriginal kings of Arcadia. Callisto, the daughter of the
wicked Lycaon, and the mother, by Zeus, of Arcas, from whom
the Arcadians took their name, was the granddaughter of
Pelasgus. The birth of Arcas brought upon Callisto the anger
of the virgin-goddess Artemis, whose service she followed: she
was changed into a she-bear, and in this form was chased by
her own son, grown to manhood. Zeus interposed, and the
mother and son were removed from the earth, and placed
among the stars. Callisto became the famous constellation of
the Great Bear; her son became Arcturus, Arctophylax, or
Boötes. From this son of Callisto were descended Cypselus,
the maternal grandfather of Æpytus, and the children of
Cypselus, Laias and Merope.

The story of the life of Hercules, the paternal ancestor of
Æpytus, is so well known that there is no need to record it.
The reader will remember that, although entitled to the throne
of Argos by right of descent from Perseus and Danaus, and
to the thrones of Sparta and Messenia by right of conquest,
Hercules yet passed his life in labours and wanderings, sub-
jected by the decree of fate to the commands of his kinsman,
the feeble and malignant Eurystheus. At his death he be-
queathed to his offspring, the Heracleidæ, his own claims to

the kingdoms of Peloponnesus, and to the persecution of Eurystheus. They at first sought shelter with Ceyx, king of Trachis; he was too weak to protect them, and they then took refuge at Athens. The Athenians refused to deliver them up at the demand of Eurystheus; he invaded Attica, and a battle was fought near Marathon, in which, after Macaria, a daughter of Hercules, had devoted herself for the preservation of her house, Eurystheus fell, and the Heracleidæ and their Athenian protectors were victorious. The memory of Macaria's self-sacrifice was perpetuated by the name of a spring of water on the plain of Marathon, the spring Macaria. The Heracleidæ then endeavoured to effect their return to Peloponnesus. Hyllus, the eldest of them, inquired of the oracle at Delphi respecting their return; he was told to return by the *narrow passage*, and in the *third harvest*. Accordingly, in the third year from that time, Hyllus led an army to the Isthmus of Corinth; but there he was encountered by an army of Achaians and Arcadians, and fell in single combat with Echemus, king of Tegea. Upon this defeat the Heracleidæ retired to Northern Greece; there, after much wandering, they finally took refuge with Ægimius, king of the Dorians, who appears to have been the fastest friend of their house, and whose Dorian warriors formed the army which at last achieved their return. But, for a hundred years from the date of their first attempt, the Heracleidæ were defeated in their successive invasions of Peloponnesus. Cleolaus and Aristomachus, the son and grandson of Hyllus, fell in unsuccessful expeditions. At length the sons of Aristomachus, Temenus, Cresphontes, and Aristodemus, when grown up, repaired to Delphi and taxed the oracle with the non-fulfilment of the promise made to their ancestor Hyllus. But Apollo replied that his oracle had been misunderstood; for that by the *third harvest* he had meant the third generation, and by the *narrow passage* he had meant the straits of the Corinthian Gulf. After this explanation the sons of Aristomachus built a fleet at Naupactus; and finally, in the hundredth year from the death of Hyllus and the eightieth from the fall of Troy, the invasion was again attempted and was this time successful. The son of Orestes, Tisamenus, who ruled both Argos and Lacedæmon, fell in battle; many of his vanquished subjects left their homes and took refuge in Achaia.

The spoil was now to be divided among the conquerors. Aristodemus, the youngest of the sons of Aristomachus, did not survive to enjoy his share. He was slain at Delphi by the sons of Pylades and Electra, the kinsmen, through their mother, of the house of Agamemnon, that house which the Heracleidæ with their Dorian army had dispossessed. The claims of Aristodemus descended to his two sons, Procles and Eurysthenes, children under the guardianship of their maternal uncle, Theras. Temenus, the eldest of the sons of Aristomachus, took the kingdom of Argos. For the two remaining kingdoms, that of Sparta and that of Messenia, his two nephews, who were to rule jointly, and their uncle Cresphontes, had to cast lots. Cresphontes wished to have the fertile Messenia, and induced his brother to acquiesce in a trick which secured it to him. The lot of Cresphontes and that of his two nephews were to be placed in a water-jar, and thrown out. Messenia was to belong to him whose lot came out first. With the connivance of Temenus, Cresphontes marked as his own lot a pellet composed of baked clay, as the lot of his nephews, a pellet of unbaked clay; the unbaked pellet was of course dissolved in the water, while the brick pellet fell out alone. Messenia, therefore, was assigned to Cresphontes.

Messenia was at this time ruled by Melanthus, a descendant of Neleus. This ancestor, a prince of the great house of Æolus, had come from Thessaly and succeeded to the Messenian throne on the failure of the previous dynasty. Melanthus and his race were thus foreigners in Messenia and were unpopular. His subjects offered little or no opposition to the invading Dorians; Melanthus abandoned his kingdom to Cresphontes, and retired to Athens.

Cresphontes married Merope, whose native country, Arcadia, was not affected by the Dorian invasion. This marriage, the issue of which was three sons, connected him with the native population of Peloponnesus. He built a new capital of Messenia, Stenyclaros, and transferred thither, from Pylos, the seat of government; he proposed, moreover, says Pausanias, to divide Messenia into five states, and to confer on the native Messenians equal privileges with their Dorian conquerors. The Dorians complained that his administration unduly favoured the vanquished people; his chief magnates, headed by Polyphontes, himself a descendant of Hercules, formed a cabal against him, and he was slain with his two eldest sons. The youngest son of Cresphontes, Æpytus, then an infant, was saved by his mother, who sent him to her father, Cypselus, the king of Arcadia, under whose protection he was brought up.

The drama begins at the moment when Æpytus, grown to manhood, returns secretly to Messenia to take vengeance on his father's murderers. At this period Temenus was no longer reigning at Argos; he had been murdered by his sons, jealous of their brother-in-law, Deiphontes. The sons of Aristodemus, Procles and Eurysthenes, at variance with their uncle and ex-guardian, Theras, were reigning at Sparta.

## PERSONS OF THE DRAMA.

LAIAS, *uncle of* ÆPYTUS, *brother of* MEROPE.

ÆPYTUS, *son of* MEROPE *and* CRESPHONTES.

POLYPHONTES, *king of* MESSENIA.

MEROPE, *widow of* CRESPHONTES, *the murdered king
of* MESSENIA.

THE CHORUS, *of* MESSENIAN *maidens.*

ARCAS, *an old man of* MEROPE's *household.*

MESSENGER.

GUARDS, ATTENDANTS, &c.

*The Scene is before the royal palace in* STENYCLAROS, *the capital
of* MESSENIA. *In the foreground is the tomb of* CRESPHONTES
*The action commences at day-break.*

# MEROPE.

LAIAS.   ÆPYTUS.

### Laias.

Son of Cresphontes, we have reach'd the goal
Of our night-journey, and thou see'st thy home.
Behold thy heritage, thy father's realm!
This is that fruitful, famed Messenian land,
Wealthy in corn and flocks, which, when at last
The late-relenting Gods with victory brought
The Heracleidæ back to Pelops' isle,
Fell to thy father's lot, the second prize.
Before thy feet this recent city spreads
Of Stenyclaros, which he built, and made
Of his fresh-conquer'd realm the royal seat,
Degrading Pylos from its ancient rule.
There stands the temple of thine ancestor,
Great Heracles; and, in that public place,
Zeus hath his altar, where thy father fell.
Southward and west, behold those snowy peaks,

Taygetus, Laconia's border-wall;
And, on this side, those confluent streams which make
Pamisus watering the Messenian plain;
Then to the north, Lycæus and the hills
Of pastoral Arcadia, where, a babe
Snatch'd from the slaughter of thy father's house,
Thy mother's kin received thee, and rear'd up.—
Our journey is well made, the work remains
Which to perform we made it; means for that
Let us consult, before this palace sends
Its inmates on their daily tasks abroad.
Haste and advise, for day comes on apace.

*Æpytus.*

O brother of my mother, guardian true,
And second father from that hour when first
My mother's faithful servant laid me down,
An infant, at the hearth of Cypselus,
My grandfather, the good Arcadian king—
Thy part it were to advise, and mine to obey.
But let us keep that purpose, which, at home,
We judged the best; chance finds no better way
Go thou into the city, and seek out
Whate'er in the Messenian people stirs
Of faithful fondness for their former king

Or hatred to their present; in this last
Will lie, my grandsire said, our fairest chance.
For tyrants make man good beyond himself;
Hate to their rule, which else would die away,
Their daily-practised chafings keep alive.
Seek this! revive, unite it, give it hope;
Bid it rise boldly at the signal given.
Meanwhile within my father's palace I,
An unknown guest, will enter, bringing word
Of my own death—but, Laias, well I hope
Through that pretended death to live and reign.

[THE CHORUS *comes forth.*

Softly, stand back!—see, to these palace gates
What black procession slowly makes approach?—
Sad-chanting maidens clad in mourning robes,
With pitchers in their hands, and fresh-pull'd flowers—
Doubtless, they bear them to my father's tomb.

[MEROPE *comes forth.*

And look, to meet them, that one, grief-plunged Form,
Severer, paler, statelier than they all,
A golden circlet on her queenly brow!
O Laias, Laias, let the heart speak here—
Shall I not greet her? shall I not leap forth?

[POLYPHONTES *comes forth, following* MEROPE.

*Laias.*

Not so! thy heart would pay its moment's speech
By silence ever after, for, behold!
The King (I know him, even through many years)
Follows the approaching Queen, who stops, as call'd
No lingering now! straight to the city I;
Do thou, till for thine entrance to this house
The happy moment comes, lurk here unseen
Behind the shelter of thy father's tomb;
Remove yet further off, if aught comes near.
But, here while harbouring, on its margin lay,
Sole offering that thou hast, locks from thy head;
And fill thy leisure with an earnest prayer
To his avenging Shade, and to the Gods
Who under earth watch guilty deeds of men,
To guide our vengeance to a prosperous close.

[LAIAS *goes out.* POLYPHONTES, MEROPE, *and*
THE CHORUS *come forward. As they advance,*
ÆPYTUS, *who at first conceals himself behind the*
*tomb, moves off the stage.*

*Polyphontes.* (*To* THE CHORUS.)

Set down your pitchers, maidens, and fall back!
Suspend your melancholy rites awhile;
Shortly ye shall resume them with your Queen.—

### (*To* MEROPE.)

I sought thee, Merope; I find thee thus,
As I have ever found thee; bent to keep,
By sad observances and public grief,
A mournful feud alive, which else would die.
I blame thee not, I do thy heart no wrong!
Thy deep seclusion, thine unyielding gloom,
Thine attitude of cold, estranged reproach,
These punctual funeral honours, year by year
Repeated, are in thee, I well believe,
Courageous, faithful actions, nobly dared.
But, Merope, the eyes of other men
Read in these actions, innocent in thee,
Perpetual promptings to rebellious hope,
War-cries to faction, year by year renew'd,
Beacons of vengeance, not to be let die.
And me, believe it, wise men gravely blame,
And ignorant men despise me, that I stand
Passive, permitting thee what course thou wilt.
Yes, the crowd mutters that remorseful fear
And paralysing conscience stop my arm,
When it should pluck thee from thy hostile way.
All this I bear, for, what I seek, I know:
Peace, peace is what I seek, and public calm;

Endless extinction of unhappy hates,
Union cemented for this nation's weal.
And even now, if to behold me here,
This day, amid these rites, this black-robed train,
Wakens, O Queen ! remembrance in thy heart
Too wide at variance with the peace I seek—
I will not violate thy noble grief,
The prayer I came to urge I will defer.

*Merope.*

This day, to-morrow, yesterday, alike
I am, I shall be, have been, in my mind
Tow'rd thee ; toward thy silence as thy speech.
Speak, therefore, or keep silence, which thou wilt.

*Polyphontes.*

Hear me, then, speak ; and let this mournful day,
The twentieth anniversary of strife,
Henceforth be honour'd as the date of peace.
Yes, twenty years ago this day beheld
The king Cresphontes, thy great husband, fall ;
It needs no yearly offerings at his tomb
To keep alive that memory in my heart—
It lives, and, while I see the light, will live.
For we were kinsmen—more than kinsmen—friends ;

Together we had grown, together lived;
Together to this isle of Pelops came
To take the inheritance of Heracles,
Together won this fair Messenian land—
Alas, that, how to rule it, was our broil!
He had his counsel, party, friends—I mine;
He stood by what he wish'd for—I the same;
I smote him, when our wishes clash'd in arms—
He had smit me, had he been swift as I.
But while I smote him, Queen, I honour'd him;
Me, too, had he prevail'd, he had not scorn'd.
Enough of this!   Since that, I have maintain'd
The sceptre—not remissly let it fall—
And I am seated on a prosperous throne;
Yet still, for I conceal it not, ferments
In the Messenian people what remains
Of thy dead husband's faction—vigorous once,
Now crush'd but not quite lifeless by his fall.
And these men look to thee, and from thy grief—
Something too studiously, forgive me, shown—
Infer thee their accomplice; and they say
That thou in secret nurturest up thy son,
Him whom thou hiddest when thy husband fell,
To avenge that fall, and bring them back to power.
Such are their hopes—I ask not if by thee

Willingly fed or no—their most vain hopes;
For I have kept conspiracy fast-chain'd
Till now, and I have strength to chain it still
But, Merope, the years advance ;—I stand
Upon the threshold of old age, alone,
Always in arms, always in face of foes.
The long repressive attitude of rule
Leaves me austerer, sterner, than I would ;
Old age is more suspicious than the free
And valiant heart of youth, or manhood's firm
Unclouded reason ; I would not decline
Into a jealous tyrant, scourged with fears,
Closing in blood and gloom his sullen reign.
The cares which might in me with time, I feel,
Beget a cruel temper, help me quell !
The breach between our parties help me close !
Assist me to rule mildly ; let us join
Our hands in solemn union, making friends
Our factions with the friendship of their chiefs.
Let us in marriage, King and Queen, unite
Claims ever hostile else, and set thy son—
No more an exile fed on empty hopes,
And to an unsubstantial title heir,
But prince adopted by the will of power,
And future king—before this people's eyes.

Consider him! consider not old hates!
Consider, too, this people, who were dear
To their dead king, thy husband—yea, too dear,
For that destroy'd him.   Give them peace! thou
    can'st.
O Merope, how many noble thoughts,
How many precious feelings of man's heart,
How many loves, how many gratitudes,
Do twenty years wear out, and see expire!
Shall they not wear one hatred out as well?

*Merope.*

Thou hast forgot, then, who I am who hear,
And who thou art who speakest to me?   I
Am Merope, thy murder'd master's wife;
And thou art Polyphontes, first his friend,
And then . . . his murderer.   These offending tears
That murder moves; this breach that thou would'st
    close
Was by that murder open'd; that one child
(If still, indeed, he lives) whom thou would'st seat
Upon a throne not thine to give, is heir,
Because thou slew'st his brothers with their father.
Who can patch union here?   What can there be
But everlasting horror 'twixt us two,

Gulfs of estranging blood?    Across that chasm
Who can extend their hands? . . . Maidens, take back
These offerings home! our rites are spoil'd to-day.


*Polyphontes.*

Not so; let these Messenian maidens mark
The fear'd and blacken'd ruler of their race,
Albeit with lips unapt to self-excuse,
Blow off the spot of murder from his name.—
Murder!—but what *is* murder?   When a wretch
For private gain or hatred takes a life,
We call it murder, crush him, brand his name.
But when, for some great public cause, an arm
Is, without love or hate, austerely raised
Against a power exempt from common checks,
Dangerous to all, to be but thus annull'd—
Ranks any man with murder such an act?
With grievous deeds, perhaps; with murder, no!
Find then such cause, the charge of murder falls—
Be judge thyself if it abound not here.
All know how weak the eagle, Heracles,
Soaring from his death-pile on Œta, left
His puny, callow eaglets; and what trials —
Infirm protectors, dubious oracles
Construed awry, misplann'd invasions—wore

Three generations of his offspring out;
Hardly the fourth, with grievous loss, regain'd
Their fathers' realm, this isle, from Pelops named.
Who made that triumph, though deferr'd, secure?
Who, but the kinsmen of the royal brood
Of Heracles, scarce Heracleidæ less
Than they? these, and the Dorian lords, whose king
Ægimius gave our outcast house a home
When Thebes, when Athens dared not; who in arms
Thrice issued with us from their pastoral vales,
And shed their blood like water in our cause?
Such were the dispossessors; of what stamp
Were they we dispossessed?—of us I speak,
Who to Messenia with thy husband came;
I speak not now of Argos, where his brother,
Not now of Sparta, where his nephews reign'd.—
What we found here were tribes of fame obscure,
Much turbulence, and little constancy,
Precariously ruled by foreign lords
From the Æolian stock of Neleus sprung,
A house once great, now dwindling in its sons.
Such were the conquer'd, such the conquerors; who
Had most thy husband's confidence? Consult
His acts! the wife he chose was—full of virtues—
But an Arcadian princess, more akin

To his new subjects than to us; his friends
Were the Messenian chiefs; the laws he framed
Were aim'd at their promotion, our decline.
And, finally, this land, then half-subdued,
Which from one central city's guarded seat
As from a fastness in the rocks our scant
Handful of Dorian conquerors might have curb'd,
He parcell'd out in five confederate states,
Sowing his victors thinly through them all,
Mere prisoners, meant or not, among our foes.
If this was fear of them, it shamed the king;
If jealousy of us, it shamed the man.
Long we refrain'd ourselves, submitted long,
Construed his acts indulgently, revered,
Though found perverse, the blood of Heracles;
Reluctantly the rest—but, against all,
One voice preach'd patience, and that voice was
        mine!
At last it reach'd us, that he, still mistrustful,
Deeming, as tyrants deem, our silence hate,
Unadulating grief conspiracy,
Had to this city, Stenyclaros, call'd
A general assemblage of the realm,
With compact in that concourse to deliver,
For death, his ancient to his new-made friends.

Patience was thenceforth self-destruction.   I,
I his chief kinsman, I his pioneer
And champion to the throne, I honouring most
Of men the line of Heracles, preferr'd
The many of that lineage to the one;
What his foes dared not, I, his lover, dared;
I at that altar, where mid shouting crowds
He sacrificed, our ruin in his heart,
To Zeus, before he struck his blow, struck mine—
Struck once, and awed his mob, and saved this realm.
Murder let others call this, if they will;
I, self-defence and righteous execution.

*Merope.*

Alas, how fair a colour can his tongue,
Who self-exculpates, lend to foulest deeds!
Thy trusting lord didst thou, his servant, slay;
Kinsman, thou slew'st thy kinsman; friend, thy
    friend—
This were enough; but let me tell thee, too,
Thou hadst no cause, as feign'd, in his misrule.
For ask at Argos, ask in Lacedæmon,
Whose people, when the Heracleidæ came,
Were hunted out, and to Achaia fled,
Whether is better, to abide alone,

A wolfish band, in a dispeopled realm,
Or conquerors with conquer'd to unite
Into one puissant folk, as he design'd ?
These sturdy and unworn Messenian tribes,
Who shook the fierce Neleidæ on their throne,
Who to the invading Dorians stretch'd a hand,
And half bestow'd, half yielded up their soil—
He would not let his savage chiefs alight,
A cloud of vultures, on this vigorous race,
Ravin a little while in spoil and blood,
Then, gorged and helpless, be assail'd and slain.
He would have saved you from your furious selves,
Not in abhorr'd estrangement let you stand ;
He would have mix'd you with your friendly foes,
Foes dazzled with your prowess, well inclined
To reverence your lineage, more, to obey ;
So would have built you, in a few short years,
A just, therefore a safe, supremacy.
For well he knew, what you, his chiefs, did not—
How of all human rules the over-tense
Are apt to snap ; the easy-stretch'd endure.
O gentle wisdom, little understood !
O arts above the vulgar tyrant's reach !
O policy too subtle far for sense
Of heady, masterful, injurious men !

This good he meant you, and for this he died!
Yet not for this—else might thy crime in part
Be error deem'd—but that pretence is vain.
For, if ye slew him for supposed misrule,
Injustice to his kin and Dorian friends,
Why with the offending father did ye slay
Two unoffending babes, his innocent sons?
Why not on them have placed the forfeit crown,
Ruled in their name, and train'd them to your will?
Had *they* misruled? had *they* forgot their friends,
Forsworn their blood? ungratefully had *they*
Preferr'd Messenian serfs to Dorian lords?
No! but to thy ambition their poor lives
Were bar—and this, too, was their father's crime.
That thou might'st reign he died, not for his fault
Even fancied; and his death thou wroughtest chief!
For, if the other lords desired his fall
Hotlier than thou, and were by thee kept back,
Why dost thou only profit by his death?
Thy crown condemns thee, while thy tongue absolves.
And now to me thou tenderest friendly league,
And to my son reversion to thy throne!
Short answer is sufficient; league with thee,
For me I deem such impious; and for him
Exile abroad more safe than heirship here.

### Polyphontes.

I ask thee not to approve thy husband's death,
No, nor expect thee to admit the grounds,
In reason good, which justified my deed.
With women the heart argues, not the mind.
But, for thy children's death, I stand assoil'd—
I saved them, meant them honour; but thy friends
Rose, and with fire and sword assailed my house
By night; in that blind tumult they were slain.
To chance impute their deaths, then, not to me.

### Merope.

Such chance as kill'd the father, kill'd the sons.

### Polyphontes.

One son at least I spared, for still he lives.

### Merope.

Tyrants think him they murder not they spare.

### Polyphontes.

Not much a tyrant thy free speech displays me.

### Merope.

Thy shame secures my freedom, not thy will.

*Polyphontes.*

Shame rarely checks the genuine tyrant's will.

*Merope.*

One merit, then, thou hast; exult in that.

*Polyphontes.*

Thou standest out, I see, repellest peace.

*Merope.*

Thy sword repell'd it long ago, not I.

*Polyphontes.*

Doubtless thou reckonest on the help of friends.

*Merope.*

Not help of men, although, perhaps, of Gods.

*Polyphontes.*

What Gods? the Gods of concord, civil weal?

*Merope.*

No! the avenging Gods, who punish crime.

### *Polyphontes.*

Beware! from thee upbraidings I receive
With pity, nay, with reverence; yet, beware!
I know, I know how hard it is to think
That right, that conscience pointed to a deed,
Where interest seems to have enjoin'd it too.
Most men are led by interest; and the few
Who are not, expiate the general sin,
Involved in one suspicion with the base.
Dizzy the path and perilous the way
Which in a deed like mine a just man treads,
But it is sometimes trodden, oh! believe it.
Yet how *canst* thou believe it? therefore thou
Hast all impunity.   Yet, lest thy friends,
Embolden'd by my lenience, think it fear,
And count on like impunity, and rise,
And have to thank thee for a fall, beware!
To rule this kingdom I intend; with sway
Clement, if may be, but to rule it—there
Expect no wavering, no retreat, no change.
And now I leave thee to these rites, esteem'd
Pious, but impious, surely, if their scope
Be to foment old memories of wrath.
Pray, as thou pour'st libations on this tomb,

To be deliver'd from thy foster'd hate,
Unjust suspicion, and erroneous fear.

    [POLYPHONTES *goes into the palace.* THE CHORUS
       *and* MEROPE *approach the tomb with their*
       *offerings.*

*The Chorus.*

Draw, draw near to the tomb !          *strophe.*
Lay honey-cakes on its marge,
Pour the libation of milk,
Deck it with garlands of flowers.
Tears fall thickly the while !
Behold, O King from the dark
House of the grave, what we do !

O Arcadian hills,          *antistrophe.*
Send us the Youth whom ye hide,
Girt with his coat for the chase,
With the low broad hat of the tann'd
Hunter o'ershadowing his brow ;
Grasping firm, in his hand
Advanced, two javelins, not now
Dangerous alone to the deer !

*Merope.*

What shall I bear, O lost          *str.* 1.
Husband and King, to thy grave ?—

Pure libations, and fresh
Flowers?   But thou, in the gloom.
Discontented, perhaps,
Demandest vengeance, not grief?
Sternly requirest a man,
Light to spring up to thy house?


### The Chorus.

Vengeance, O Queen, is his due,                    *str. 2.*
His most just prayer; yet his house—
If that might soothe him below—
Prosperous, mighty, came back
In the third generation, the way
Order'd by Fate, to their home;
And now, glorious, secure,
Fill the wealth-giving thrones
Of their heritage, Pelops' isle.


### Merope.

Suffering sent them, Death                    *ant. 1.*
March'd with them, Hatred and Strife
Met them entering their halls.
For from the day when the first
Heracleidæ received
That Delphic hest to return,

What hath involved them, but blind
Error on error, and blood?

### The Chorus.

Truly I hear of a Maid                    *ant. 2.*
Of that stock born, who bestow'd
Her blood that so she might make
Victory sure to her race,
When the fight hung in doubt! but she now,
Honour'd and sung of by all,
Far on Marathon plain,
Gives her name to the spring
Macaria, blessed Child.

### Merope.

She led the way of death.                    *str. 3*
And the plain of Tegea,
And the grave of Orestes—
Where, in secret seclusion
Of his unreveal'd tomb,
Sleeps Agamemnon's unhappy,
Matricidal, world-famed,
Seven-cubit-statured son—
Sent forth Echemus, the victor, the king,
By whose hand, at the Isthmus,

At the fate-denied straits,
Fell the eldest of the sons of Heracles,
Hyllus, the chief of his house.
Brother follow'd sister
The all-wept way.

### The Chorus.

Yes; but his seed still, wiser-counsell'd,
Sail'd by the fate-meant Gulf to their conquest—
Slew their enemies' king, Tisamenus.
Wherefore accept that happier omen!
Yet shall restorer appear to the race.

### Merope.

Three brothers won the field,                    *ant.* 3
And to two did Destiny
Give the thrones that they conquer'd.
But the third, what delays him
From his unattain'd crown? . . .
Ah Pylades and Electra,
Ever faithful, untired,
Jealous, blood-exacting friends!
Your sons leap upon the foe of your kin.
In the passes of Delphi,
In the temple-built gorge!

There the youngest of the band of conquerors
Perish'd, in sight of the goal.
Thrice son follow'd sire
The all-wept way.

### The Chorus.

Thou tellest the fate of the last        *str.* 4.
Of the three Heracleidæ.
Not of him, of Cresphontes thou shared'st the lot!
A king, a king was he while he lived,
Swaying the sceptre with predestined hand;
And now, minister loved,
Holds rule.

### Merope.

Ah me . . . Ah . . .

### The Chorus.

For the awful Monarchs below.

### Merope.

Thou touchest the worst of my ills.        *str.* 5
Oh had he fallen of old
At the Isthmus, in fight with his foes,
By Achaian, Arcadian spear!
Then had his sepulchre risen

On the high sea-bank, in the sight
Of either Gulf, and remain'd
All-regarded afar,
Noble memorial of worth
Of a valiant Chief, to his own.

### The Chorus.

There rose up a cry in the streets                    *ant.* 4
From the terrified people.
From the altar of Zeus, from the crowd, came a wail
A blow, a blow was struck, and he fell,
Sullying his garment with dark-streaming blood ;
While stood o'er him a Form—
Some Form

### Merope.

Ah me . . . Ah . . .

### The Chorus.

Of a dreadful Presence of fear.

### Merope.

More piercing the second cry rang,                    *ant.* 5.
Wail'd from the palace within,
From the Children. . . . The Fury to them,
Fresh from their father, draws near.

Ah bloody axe! dizzy blows!
In these ears, they thunder, they ring,
These poor ears, still! and these eyes
Night and day see them fall,
Fiery phantoms of death,
On the fair, curl'd heads of my sons.

### The Chorus.

Not to thee only hath come      *str.* 6.
Sorrow, O Queen, of mankind.
Had not Electra to haunt
A palace defiled by a death unavenged,
For years, in silence, devouring her heart?
But her nursling, her hope, came at last.
Thou, too, rearest in hope,
Far 'mid Arcadian hills,
Somewhere, for vengeance, a champion, a light.
Soon, soon shall Zeus bring him home!
Soon shall he dawn on this land!

### Merope.

Him in secret, in tears,      *str* 7.
Month after month, I await
Vainly. For he, in the glens
Of Lycæus afar,

III                 D

A gladsome hunter of deer,
Basks in his morning of youth,
Spares not a thought to his home.


### The Chorus.

Give not thy heart to despair.                    *ant.* 6.
No lamentation can loose
Prisoners of death from the grave ;
But Zeus, who accounteth thy quarrel his own,
Still rules, still watches, and numb'reth the hours
Till the sinner, the vengeance, be ripe.
Still, by Acheron stream,
Terrible Deities throned
Sit, and eye grimly the victim unscourged.
Still, still the Dorian boy,
Exiled, remembers his home.


### Merope.

Him if high-ruling Zeus                           *ant.* 7
Bring to me safe, let the rest
Go as it will !   But if this
Clash with justice, the Gods
Forgive my folly, and work
Vengeance on sinner and sin—
Only to me give my child !

#### The Chorus.

Hear us and help us, Shade of our King !          *str.* 8.

#### Merope.

A return, O Father ! give to thy boy !          *str.* 9.

#### The Chorus.

Send an avenger, Gods of the dead !          *ant.* 8.

#### Merope.

An avenger I ask not—send me my son !          *ant.* 9

#### The Chorus.

O Queen, for an avenger to appear,
Thinking that so I pray'd aright, I pray'd ;
If I pray'd wrongly, I revoke the prayer.

#### Merope.

Forgive me, maidens, if I seem too slack
In calling vengeance on a murderer's head.
Impious I deem the alliance which he asks,
Requite him words severe for seeming kind,
And righteous, if he falls, I count his fall.
With this, to those unbribed inquisitors
Who in man's inmost bosom sit and judge,
The true avengers these, I leave his deed,

By him shown fair, but, I believe, most foul.
If these condemn him, let them pass his doom!
That doom obtain effect, from Gods or men!
So be it; yet will that more solace bring
To the chafed heart of Justice than to mine.
To hear another tumult in these streets,
To have another murder in these halls,
To see another mighty victim bleed—
Small comfort offers for a woman there!
A woman, O my friends, has one desire:
To see secure, to live with, those she loves.
Can vengeance give me back the murdered? no!
Can it bring home my child? Ah, if it can,
I pray the Furies' ever-restless band,
And pray the Gods, and pray the all-seeing sun:
"Sun, who careerest through the height of Heaven,
When o'er the Arcadian forests thou art come,
And see'st my stripling hunter there afield,
Put tightness in thy gold-embossed rein,
And check thy fiery steeds, and, leaning back,
Throw him a pealing word of summons down,
To come, a late avenger, to the aid
Of this poor soul who bare him, and his sire."
If this will bring him back, be this my prayer!
But Vengeance travels in a dangerous way,

Double of issue, full of pits and snares
For all who pass, pursuers and pursued—
That way is dubious for a mother's prayer.
Rather on thee I call, Husband beloved—
May Hermes, herald of the dead, convey
My words below to thee, and make thee hear—
Bring back our son! if may be, without blood!
Install him in thy throne, still without blood!
Grant him to reign there wise and just like thee,
More fortunate than thee, more fairly judged!
This for our son; and for myself I pray,
Soon, having once beheld him, to descend
Into the quiet gloom, where thou art now.
These words to thine indulgent ear, thy wife,
I send, and these libations pour the while.

[*They make their offerings at the tomb.* MEROPE
*then turns to go towards the palace.*

### The Chorus.

The dead hath now his offerings duly paid.
But whither go'st thou hence, O Queen, away?

### Merope.

To receive Arcas, who to-day should come,
Bringing me of my boy the annual news.

*The Chorus.*

No certain news if like the rest it run.

*Merope.*

Certain in this, that 'tis uncertain still.

*The Chorus.*

What keeps him in Arcadia from return ?

*Merope.*

His grandsire and his uncles fear the risk.

*The Chorus.*

Of what ? it lies with them to make risk none.

*Merope.*

Discovery of a visit made by stealth.

*The Chorus.*

With arms then they should send him, not by stealth

*Merope.*

With arms they dare not, and by stealth they fear.

*The Chorus.*

I doubt their caution little suits their ward.

*Merope.*

The heart of youth I know; that most I fear.

*The Chorus.*

I augur thou wilt hear some bold resolve.

*Merope.*

I dare not wish it; but, at least, to hear
That my son still survives, in health, in bloom;
To hear that still he loves, still longs for, me,
Yet, with a light uncareworn spirit, turns
Quick from distressful thought, and floats in joy—
Thus much from Arcas, my old servant true,
Who saved him from these murderous halls a babe,
And since has fondly watch'd him night and day
Save for this annual charge, I hope to hear.
If this be all, I know not; but I know,
These many years I live for this alone.

[MEROPE *goes in.*

*The Chorus.*

Much is there which the sea                  *str.* 1.
Conceals from man, who cannot plumb its depths.
Air to his unwing'd form denies a way,

And keeps its liquid solitudes unscaled.
Even earth, whereon he treads,
So feeble is his march, so slow,
Holds countless tracts untrod.

But more than all unplumb'd,                    *ant.* 1
Unscaled, untrodden, is the heart of man.
More than all secrets hid, the way it keeps.
Nor any of our organs so obtuse,
Inaccurate, and frail,
As those wherewith we try to test
Feelings and motives there.

Yea, and not only have we not explored          *str.* 2
That wide and various world, the heart of others,
But even our own heart, that narrow world
Bounded in our own breast, we hardly know,
Of our own actions dimly trace the causes.
Whether a natural obscureness, hiding
That region in perpetual cloud,
Or our own want of effort, be the bar.

Therefore—while acts are from their motives
        judged,                                 *ant.* 2
And to one act many most unlike motives,

This pure, that guilty, may have each impell'd—
Power fails us to try clearly if that cause
Assign'd us by the actor be the true one;
Power fails the man himself to fix distinctly
The cause which drew him to his deed,
And stamp himself, thereafter, bad or good.

*The most are bad*, wise men have said.       *str.* 3
*Let the best rule*, they say again.
The best, then, to dominion hath the right.
Rights unconceded and denied,
Surely, if rights, may be by force asserted—
May be, nay should, if for the general weal.
The best, then, to the throne may carve his way,
And strike opposers down,
Free from all guilt of lawlessness,
Or selfish lust of personal power;
Bent only to serve virtue,
Bent to diminish wrong.

And truly, in this ill-ruled world,       *ant.* 3
Well sometimes may the good desire
To give to virtue her dominion due!
Well may he long to interrupt
The reign of folly, usurpation ever,

Though fenced by sanction of a thousand years !
Well thirst to drag the wrongful ruler down ;
Well purpose to pen back
Into the narrow path of right
The ignorant, headlong multitude,
Who blindly follow, ever,
Blind leaders, to their bane !

But who can say, without a fear :          *str* 4
*That best, who ought to rule, am I ;*
*The mob, who ought to obey, are these ;*
*I the one righteous, they the many bad ?*
Who, without check of conscience, can aver
That he to power makes way by arms,
Sheds blood, imprisons, banishes, attaints,
Commits all deeds the guilty oftenest do,
Without a single guilty thought,
Arm'd for right only, and the general good ?

Therefore, with censure unallay'd,          *ant.* 4.
Therefore, with unexcepting ban,
Zeus and pure-thoughted Justice brand
Imperious self-asserting violence ;
Sternly condemn the too bold man, who dares
Elect himself Heaven's destined arm ;

And, knowing well man's inmost heart infirm,
However noble the committer be,
His grounds however specious shown,
Turn with averted eyes from deeds of blood.

Thus, though a woman, I was school'd      *epode*
By those whom I revere.
Whether I learnt their lessons well,
Or, having learnt them, well apply
To what hath in this house befall'n,
If in the event be any proof,
The event will quickly show.

           [ÆPYTUS *comes in*

### *Æpytus.*

Maidens, assure me if they told me true
Who told me that the royal house was here.

### *The Chorus.*

Rightly they told thee, and thou art arrived.

### *Æpytus.*

Here, then, it is, where Polyphontes dwells?

### *The Chorus.*

He doth; thou hast both house and master right.

*Æpytus.*

Might some one straight inform him he is sought?

*The Chorus.*

Inform him that thyself, for here he comes.

[POLYPHONTES *comes forth, with* ATTENDANTS
       *and* GUARDS.

*Æpytus.*

O King, all hail! I come with weighty news;
Most likely, grateful; but, in all case, sure.

*Polyphontes.*

Speak them, that I may judge their kind myself.

*Æpytus.*

Accept them in one word, for good or bad:
Æpytus, the Messenian prince, is dead!

*Polyphontes.*

Dead!—and when died he? where? and by what
       hand?
And who art thou, who bringest me such news?

College of the Pacific
Stockton, Calif.

*Æpytus.*

He perish'd in Arcadia, where he dwelt
With Cypselus; and two days since he died.
One of the train of Cypselus am I.

*Polyphontes.*

Instruct me of the manner of his death.

*Æpytus.*

That will I do, and to this end I came.
For, being of like age, of birth not mean,
The son of an Arcadian noble, I
Was chosen his companion from a boy;
And on the hunting-rambles which his heart,
Unquiet, drove him ever to pursue·
Through all the lordships of the Arcadian dales,
From chief to chief, I wander'd at his side,
The captain of his squires, and his guard.
On such a hunting-journey, three morns since,
With beaters, hounds, and huntsmen, he and I
Set forth from Tegea, the royal town.
The prince at start seem'd sad, but his regard
Clear'd with blithe travel and the morning air.
We rode from Tegea, through the woods of oaks,
Past Arnê spring, where Rhea gave the babe

Poseidon to the shepherd-boys to hide
From Saturn's search among the new-yean'd lambs,
To Mantineia, with its unbaked walls;
Thence, by the Sea-God's Sanctuary and the tomb
Whither from wintry Mænalus were brought
The bones of Arcas, whence our race is named,
On, to the marshy Orchomenian plain,
And the Stone Coffins;—then, by Caphyæ Cliffs,
To Pheneos with its craggy citadel.
There, with the chief of that hill-town, we lodged
One night; and the next day at dawn fared on
By the Three Fountains and the Adder's Hill
To the Stymphalian Lake, our journey's end,
To draw the coverts on Cyllenê's side.
There, on a high green spur which bathes its point
Far in the liquid lake, we sate, and drew
Cates from our hunters' pouch, Arcadian fare,
Sweet chestnuts, barley-cakes, and boar's-flesh dried;
And as we ate, and rested there, we talk'd
Of places we had pass'd, sport we had had,
Of beasts of chase that haunt the Arcadian hills,
Wild hog, and bear, and mountain-deer, and roe;
Last, of our quarters with the Arcadian chiefs
For courteous entertainment, welcome warm,
Sad, reverential homage, had our prince

From all, for his great lineage and his woes;
All which he own'd, and praised with grateful mind
But still over his speech a gloom there hung,
As of one shadow'd by impending death;
And strangely, as we talk'd, he would apply
The story of spots mention'd to his own;
Telling us, Arnê minded him, he too
Was saved a babe, but to a life obscure,
Which he, the seed of Heracles, dragg'd on
Inglorious, and should drop at last unknown,
Even as those dead unepitaph'd, who lie
In the stone coffins at Orchomenus.
And, then, he bade remember how we pass'd
The Mantineän Sanctuary, forbid
To foot of mortal, where his ancestor,
Named Æpytus like him, having gone in,
Was blinded by the outgushing springs of brine.
Then, turning westward to the Adder's Hill—
*Another ancestor, named, too, like me,*
*Died of a snake-bite,* said he, *on that brow;*
*Still at his mountain-tomb men marvel, built*
*Where, as life ebb'd, his bearers laid him down.*
So he play'd on; then ended, with a smile:
*This region is not happy for my race.*
We cheer'd him; but, that moment, from the copse

By the lake-edge, broke the sharp cry of hounds;
The prickers shouted that the stag was gone.
We sprang upon our feet, we snatch'd our spears,
We bounded down the swarded slope, we plunged
Through the dense ilex-thickets to the dogs.
Far in the woods ahead their music rang;
And many times that morn we coursed in ring
The forests round that belt Cyllenê's side;
Till I, thrown out and tired, came to halt
On that same spur where we had sate at morn.
And resting there to breathe, I watch'd the chase—
Rare, straggling hunters, foil'd by brake and crag,
And the prince, single, pressing on the rear
Of that unflagging quarry and the hounds.
Now in the woods far down I saw them cross
An open glade; now he was high aloft
On some tall scar fringed with dark feathery pines,
Peering to spy a goat-track down the cliff,
Cheering with hand, and voice, and horn his dogs.
At last the cry drew to the water's edge—
And through the brushwood, to the pebbly strand,
Broke, black with sweat, the antler'd mountain-stag,
And took the lake.   Two hounds alone pursued,
Then came the prince; he shouted and plunged in.
—There is a chasm rifted in the base

Of that unfooted precipice, whose rock
Walls on one side the deep Stymphalian Lake;
There the lake-waters, which in ages gone
Wash'd, as the marks upon the hills still show,
All the Stymphalian plain, are now suck'd down.
A headland, with one aged plane-tree crown'd,
Parts from this cave-pierced cliff the shelving bay
Where first the chase plunged in; the bay is smooth,
But round the headland's point a current sets,
Strong, black, tempestuous, to the cavern-mouth.
Stoutly, under the headland's lee, they swam;
But when they came abreast the point, the race
Caught them as wind takes feathers, whirl'd them
     round
Struggling in vain to cross it, swept them on,
Stag, dogs, and hunter, to the yawning gulph.
All this, O King, not piecemeal, as to thee
Now told, but in one flashing instant pass'd.
While from the turf whereon I lay I sprang
And took three strides, quarry and dogs were gone;
A moment more—I saw the prince turn round
Once in the black and arrowy race, and cast
An arm aloft for help; then sweep beneath
The low-brow'd cavern-arch, and disappear.
And what I could, I did—to call by cries

Some straggling hunters to my aid, to rouse
Fishers who live on the lake-side, to launch
Boats, and approach, near as we dared, the chasm.
But of the prince nothing remain'd, save this,
His boar-spear's broken shaft, back on the lake
Cast by the rumbling subterranean stream;
And this, at landing spied by us and saved,
His broad-brimm'd hunter's hat, which, in the bay,
Where first the stag took water, floated still.
And I across the mountains brought with haste
To Cypselus, at Basilis, this news—
Basilis, his new city, which he now
Near Lycosura builds, Lycaon's town,
First city founded on the earth by men.
He to thee sends me on, in one thing glad,
While all else grieves him, that his grandchild's death
Extinguishes distrust 'twixt him and thee.
But I from our deplored mischance learn this:
The man who to untimely death is doom'd,
Vainly you hedge him from the assault of harm;
He bears the seed of ruin in himself.

### The Chorus.

So dies the last shoot of our royal tree!
Who shall tell Merope this heavy news?

*Polyphontes.*

Stranger, this news thou bringest is too great
For instant comment, having many sides
Of import, and in silence best received,
Whether it turn at last to joy or woe.
But thou, the zealous bearer, hast no part
In what it hath of painful, whether now,
First heard, or in its future issue shown.
Thou for thy labour hast deserved our best
Refreshment, needed by thee, as I judge,
With mountain-travel and night-watching spent.—
To the guest-chamber lead him, some one ! give
All entertainment which a traveller needs,
And such as fits a royal house to show ;
To friends, still more, and labourers in our cause.

[ATTENDANTS *conduct* ÆPYTUS *within the palace.*

*The Chorus.*

The youth is gone within ; alas ! he bears
A presence sad for some one through those doors.

*Polyphontes.*

Admire then, maidens, how in one short hour
The schemes, pursued in vain for twenty years,
Are—by a stroke, though undesired, complete—

Crown'd with success, not in my way, but Heaven's !
This at a moment, too, when I had urged
A last, long-cherish'd project, in my aim
Of peace, and been repulsed with hate and scorn.
Fair terms of reconcilement, equal rule,
I offer'd to my foes, and they refused ;
Worse terms than mine they have obtain'd from
  Heaven.
Dire is this blow for Merope ; and I
Wish'd, truly wish'd, solution to our broil
Other than by this death ; but it hath come !
I speak no word of boast, but this I say :
A private loss here founds a nation's peace.

      [POLYPHONTES *goes out.*

### *The Chorus.*

Peace, who tarriest too long ;     *str.*
Peace, with delight in thy train ;
Come, come back to our prayer !
Then shall the revel again
Visit our streets, and the sound
Of the harp be heard with the pipe,
When the flashing torches appear
In the marriage-train coming on,
With dancing maidens and boys—

While the matrons come to the doors,
And the old men rise from their bench,
When the youths bring home the bride.

Not condemn'd by my voice                    *ant.*
He who restores thee shall be,
Not unfavour'd by Heaven.
Surely no sinner the man,
Dread though his acts, to whose hand
Such a boon to bring hath been given.
Let her come, fair Peace! let her come!
But the demons long nourish'd here,
Murder, Discord, and Hate,
In the stormy desolate waves
Of the Thracian Sea let her leave,
Or the howling outermost main!

[MEROPE *comes forth.*

*Merope.*

A whisper through the palace flies of one
Arrived from Tegea with weighty news;
And I came, thinking to find Arcas here.
Ye have not left this gate, which he must pass;
Tell me—hath one not come? or, worse mischance,
Come, but been intercepted by the King?

*The Chorus.*

A messenger, sent from Arcadia here,
Arrived, and of the King had speech but now.

*Merope.*

Ah me ! the wrong expectant got his news.

*The Chorus.*

The message brought was for the King design'd

*Merope.*

How so ? was Arcas not the messenger?

*The Chorus.*

A younger man, and of a different name.

*Merope.*

And what Arcadian news had he to tell ?

*The Chorus.*

Learn that from other lips, O Queen, than mine.

*Merope.*

He kept his tale, then, for the King alone!

*The Chorus.*

His tale was meeter for that ear than thine.

*Merope.*

Why dost thou falter, and make half reply?

*The Chorus.*

O thrice unhappy, how I groan thy fate!

*Merope.*

Thou frightenest and confound'st me by thy words.
O were but Arcas come, all would be well?

*The Chorus.*

If so, all's well: for look, the old man speeds
Up from the city tow'rd this gated hill.

[ARCAS *comes in.*

*Merope.*

Not with the failing breath and foot of age
My faithful follower comes.   Welcome, old friend!

*Arcas.*

Faithful, not welcome, when my tale is told.
O that my over-speed and bursting grief

Had on the journey choked my labouring breath,
And lock'd my speech for ever in my breast!
Yet then another man would bring this news,
Wherewith from end to end Arcadia rings.—
O honour'd Queen, thy son, my charge, is gone.

*The Chorus.*

Too suddenly thou tellest such a loss.
Look up, O Queen! look up, O mistress dear!
Look up, and see thy friends who comfort thee.

*Merope.*

Ah . . . Ah . . . Ah me!

*The Chorus.*

And I, too, say, ah me!

*Arcas.*

Forgive, forgive the bringer of such news!

*Merope.*

Better from thine than from an enemy's tongue.

*The Chorus.*

And yet no enemy did this, O Queen:
But the wit-baffling will and hand of Heaven.

*Arcas.*

No enemy ! and what hast thou, then, heard ?
Swift as I came, hath falsehood been before ?

*The Chorus.*

A youth arrived but now—the son, he said,
Of an Arcadian lord—our prince's friend—
Jaded with travel, clad in hunter's garb.
He brought report that his own eyes had seen
The prince, in chase after a swimming stag,
Swept down a chasm rifted in the cliff
Which hangs o'er the Stymphalian Lake, and drown'd.

*Arcas.*

Ah me ! with what a foot doth treason post,
While loyalty, with all her speed, is slow !
Another tale, I trow, thy messenger
For the King's private ear reserves, like this
In one thing only, that the prince is dead.

*The Chorus.*

And how then runs this true and private tale ?

*Arcas.*

As much to the King's wish, more to his shame.
This young Arcadian noble, guard and mate

To Æpytus, the king seduced with gold,
And had him at the prince's side in leash,
Ready to slip on his unconscious prey.
He on a hunting party two days since,
Among the forests on Cyllenê's side,
Perform'd good service for his bloody wage;
Our prince, and the good Laias, whom his ward
Had in a father's place, he basely murder'd.
'Tis so, 'tis so, alas, for see the proof:
Uncle and nephew disappear; their death
Is charged against this stripling; agents, fee'd
To ply 'twixt the Messenian king and him,
Come forth, denounce the traffic and the traitor.
Seized, he escapes—and next I find him here.
Take this for true, the other tale for feign'd.

*The Chorus.*

The youth, thou say'st, we saw and heard but now—

*Arcas.*

He comes to tell his prompter he hath sped.

*The Chorus.*

Still he repeats the drowning story here.

*Arcas.*

To thee—that needs no Œdipus to explain.

*The Chorus.*

Interpret, then; for we, it seems, are dull.

*Arcas.*

Your King desired the profit of his death,
Not the black credit of his murderer.
That stern word *"murder"* had too dread a sound
For the Messenian hearts, who loved the prince.

*The Chorus.*

Suspicion grave I see, but no firm proof.

*Merope.*

Peace! peace! all's clear.—The wicked watch and
    work
While the good sleep; the workers have the day.
Yes! yes! now I conceive the liberal grace
Of this far-scheming tyrant, and his boon
Of heirship to his kingdom for my son:
He had his murderer ready, and the sword
Lifted, and that unwish'd-for heirship void—
A tale, meanwhile, forged for his subjects' ears—
And me, henceforth sole rival with himself
In their allegiance, me, in my son's death-hour,
When all turn'd tow'rds me, me he would have shown

To my Messenians, duped, disarm'd, despised,
The willing sharer of his guilty rule,
All claim to succour forfeit, to myself
Hateful, by each Messenian heart abhorr'd.
His offers I repell'd—but what of that?
If with no rage, no fire of righteous hate,
Such as ere now hath spurr'd to fearful deeds
Weak women with a thousandth part my wrongs,
But calm, but unresentful, I endured
His offers, coldly heard them, cold repell'd?
How must men think me abject, void of heart,
While all this time I bear to linger on
In this blood-deluged palace, in whose halls
Either a vengeful Fury I should stalk,
Or else not live at all!—but here I haunt,
A pale, unmeaning ghost, powerless to fright
Or harm, and nurse my longing for my son,
A helpless one, I know it—but the Gods
Have temper'd me e'en thus, and, in some souls,
Misery, which rouses others, breaks the spring.
And even now, my son, ah me! my son,
Fain would I fade away, as I have lived,
Without a cry, a struggle, or a blow,
All vengeance unattempted, and descend
To the invisible plains, to roam with thee,

Fit denizen, the lampless under-world——
But with what eyes should I encounter there
My husband, wandering with his stern compeers,
Amphiaraos, or Mycenæ's king,
Who led the Greeks to Ilium, Agamemnon,
Betray'd like him, but, not like him, avenged?
Or with what voice shall I the questions meet
Of my two elder sons, slain long ago,
Who sadly ask me, what, if not revenge,
Kept me, their mother, from their side so long?
Or how reply to thee, my child last-born,
Last-murder'd, who reproachfully wilt say ·
*Mother, I well believed thou lived'st on*
*In the detested palace of thy foe,*
*With patience on thy face, death in thy heart,*
*Counting, till I grew up, the laggard years,*
*That our joint hands might then together pay*
*To our unhappy house the debt we owe.*
*My death makes my debt void, and doubles thine—*
*But down thou fleecst here, and leav'st our scourge*
*Triumphant, and condemnest all our race*
*To lie in gloom for ever unappeased.*
What shall I have to answer to such words?—
No, something must be dared; and, great as erst
Our dastard patience, be our daring now!

Come, ye swift Furies, who to him ye haunt
Permit no peace till your behests are done;
Come Hermes, who dost friend the unjustly kill'd,
And can'st teach simple ones to plot and feign;
Come, lightning Passion, that with foot of fire
Advancest to the middle of a deed
Almost before 'tis plann'd; come, glowing Hate;
Come, baneful Mischief, from thy murky den
Under the dripping black Tartarean cliff
Which Styx's awful waters trickle down—
Inspire this coward heart, this flagging arm!
How say ye, maidens, do ye know these prayers?
Are these words Merope's—is this voice mine?
Old man, old man, thou had'st my boy in charge,
And he is lost, and thou hast that to atone!
Fly, find me on the instant where confer
The murderer and his impious setter-on—
And ye, keep faithful silence, friends, and mark
What one weak woman can achieve alone.

*Arcas.*

O mistress, by the Gods, do nothing rash!

*Merope.*

Unfaithful servant, dost thou, too, desert me?

*Arcas.*

I go! I go!—The King holds council—there
Will I seek tidings.   Take, the while, this word:
Attempting deeds beyond thy power to do,
Thou nothing profitest thy friends, but mak'st
Our misery more, and thine own ruin sure.

[ARCAS *goes out.*

*The Chorus.*

I have heard, O Queen, how a prince,          *str.* 1
Agamemnon's son, in Mycenæ,
Orestes, died but in name,
Lived for the death of his foes.

*Merope.*

Peace!

*The Chorus.*

What is it?

*Merope.*

Alas,

Thou destroyest me!

*The Chorus.*

How?

### Merope.

Whispering hope of a life
Which no stranger unknown,
But the faithful servant and nurse,
Whose tears warrant his truth,
Bears sad witness is lost.

### The Chorus.

Wheresoe'er men are, there is grief.          *ant.* 1.
In a thousand countries, a thousand
Homes, e'en now is there wail ;
Mothers lamenting their sons.

### Merope.

Yes——

### The Chorus

Thou knowest it ?

### Merope.

                    This,
Who lives, witnesses.

### The Chorus

True.

*Merope.*

But is it only a fate
Sure, all-common, to lose
In a land of friends, by a friend,
One last, murder-saved child?

*The Chorus.*

Ah me!                                    *str.* 2.

*Merope.*

Thou confessest the prize
In the rushing, thundering, mad
Cloud-enveloped, obscure,
Unapplauded, unsung
Race of calamity, mine?

*The Chorus.*

None can truly claim that
Mournful preëminence, not
Thou.

*Merope.*

Fate *gives* it, ah me!

*The Chorus.*

Not, above all, in the doubts,
Double and clashing, that hang——

III                                       F

*Merope*

What then ?                                    *ant 2*

Seems it lighter, my loss,

If, perhaps, unpierced by the sword,

My child lies in his jagg'd

Sunless prison of rock,

On the black wave borne to and fro ?

*The Chorus.*

Worse, far worse, if his friend,

If the Arcadian within,

If——

*Merope (with a start)*

How say'st thou ? within ? . . .

*The Chorus.*

He in the guest-chamber now,

Faithlessly murder'd his friend.

*Merope.*

Ye, too, ye, too, join to betray, then,

Your Queen !

*The Chorus.*

What is this ?

*Merope.*

Ye knew,

O false friends! into what
Haven the murderer had dropp'd?
Ye kept silence?

*The Chorus.*

In fear,

O loved mistress! in fear,
Dreading thine over-wrought mood,
What I knew, I conceal'd.

*Merope.*

Swear by the Gods henceforth to obey me!

*The Chorus.*

Unhappy one, what deed
Purposes thy despair?
I promise; but I fear.

*Merope.*

From the altar, the unavenged tomb,
Fetch me the sacrifice-axe!——

[THE CHORUS *goes towards the tomb of* CRES-
PHONTES, *and their leader brings back the axe.*

O Husband, O clothed
With the grave's everlasting,
All-covering darkness!   O King,
Well mourn'd, but ill-avenged!
Approv'st thou thy wife now?——
The axe!—who brings it?

### The Chorus.

'Tis here!
But thy gesture, thy look,
Appals me, shakes me with awe.

### Merope.

Thrust back now the bolt of that door!

### The Chorus.

Alas! alas!—
Behold the fastenings withdrawn
Of the guest-chamber door!—
Ah! I beseech thee—with tears——

### Merope.

Throw the door open!

### The Chorus.

'Tis done! . . .

[*The door of the house is thrown open: the interior*
*of the guest-chamber is discovered, with* ÆPYTUS
*asleep on a couch.*

### Merope.

He sleeps—sleeps calm.   O ye all-seeing Gods!
Thus peacefully do ye let sinners sleep,
While troubled innocents toss, and lie awake?
What sweeter sleep than this could I desire
For thee, my child, if thou wert yet alive?
How often have I dream'd of thee like this,
With thy soil'd hunting-coat, and sandals torn
Asleep in the Arcadian glens at noon,
Thy head droop'd softly, and the golden curls
Clustering o'er thy white forehead, like a girl's;
The short proud lip showing thy race, thy cheeks
Brown'd with thine open-air, free, hunter's life.
Ah me!
And where dost thou sleep now, my innocent
         boy?—
In some dark fir-tree's shadow, amid rocks

Untrodden, on Cyllenê's desolate side ;
Where travellers never pass, where only come
Wild beasts, and vultures sailing overhead.
There, there thou liest now, my hapless child !
Stretch'd among briars and stones, the slow, black
     gore
Oozing through thy soak'd hunting-shirt, with limbs
Yet stark from the death-struggle, tight-clench'd
     hands,
And eyeballs staring for revenge in vain.
Ah miserable !
And thou, thou fair-skinn'd Serpent ! thou art laid
In a rich chamber, on a happy bed,
In a king's house, thy victim's heritage ;
And drink'st untroubled slumber, to sleep off
The toils of thy foul service, till thou wake
Refresh'd, and claim thy master's thanks and gold.—
Wake up in hell from thine unhallow'd sleep,
Thou smiling Fiend, and claim thy guerdon there !
Wake amid gloom, and howling, and the noise
Of sinners pinion'd on the torturing wheel,
And the stanch Furies' never-silent scourge.
And bid the chief tormentors there provide
For a grand culprit shortly coming down.
Go thou the first, and usher in thy lord !

A more just stroke than that thou gav'st my son
Take——

> [MEROPE *advances towards the sleeping ÆPYTUS,*
> *with the axe uplifted.   At the same moment*
> ARCAS *re-enters.*

*Arcas (to the Chorus).*

Not with him to council did the King
Carry his messenger, but left him here.

> [*Sees* MEROPE *and* ÆPYTUS.

O Gods ! . . .

*Merope.*

Foolish old man, thou spoil'st my blow !

*Arcas.*

What do I see ? . . .

*Merope.*

A murderer at death's door.
Therefore no words !

*Arcas.*

A murderer ? . . .

*Merope.*

And a captive
To the dear next-of-kin of him he murder'd.
Stand, and let vengeance pass !

*Arcas.*

Hold, O Queen, hold !
Thou know'st not whom thou strik'st . . .

*Merope.*

I know his crime.

*Arcas.*

Unhappy one ! thou strik'st——

*Merope.*

A most just blow.

*Arcas.*

No, by the Gods, thou slay'st——

*Merope.*

Stand off !

*Arcas.*

Thy son !

*Merope.*

Ah! . . . .

[*She lets the axe drop, and falls insensible.*

*Æpytus* (*awaking*).

Who are these? What shrill, ear-piercing scream
Wakes me thus kindly from the perilous sleep
Wherewith fatigue and youth had bound mine eyes,
Even in the deadly palace of my foe?—
Arcas! Thou here?

*Arcas* (*embracing him*).

O my dear master! O
My child, my charge beloved, welcome to life!
As dead we held thee, mourn'd for thee as dead.

*Æpytus.*

In word I died, that I in deed might live.
But who are these?

*Arcas.*

Messenian maidens, friends.

*Æpytus.*

And, Arcas!—but I tremble!

*Arcas.*

Boldly ask

*Æpytus.*

That black-robed, swooning figure? . . .

*Arcas.*

Merope.

*Æpytus.*

O mother! mother!

*Merope.*

Who upbraids me?   Ah! . .

[*seeing the axe*

*Æpytus.*

Upbraids thee? no one.

*Merope.*

Thou dost well: but take . . .

*Æpytus.*

What wav'st thou off?

*Merope.*

That murderous axe away!

*Æpytus.*

Thy son is here.

*Merope.*

One said so, sure, but now.

*Æpytus.*

Here, here thou hast him!

*Merope.*

Slaughter'd by this hand! . . .

*Æpytus.*

No, by the Gods, alive and like to live!

*Merope.*

What, thou?—I dream——

*Æpytus.*

May'st thou dream ever so!

*Merope* (*advancing towards him*).

My child? unhurt? . . .

*Æpytus.*

Only by over joy

*Merope.*

Art thou, then, come ? . . .

*Æpytus.*

Never to part again.

[*They fall into one another's arms.  Then* MEROPE,
   *holding* ÆPYTUS *by the hand, turns to* THE
   CHORUS.

*Merope.*

O kind Messenian maidens, O my friends,
Bear witness, see, mark well, on what a head
My first stroke of revenge had nearly fallen !

*The Chorus.*

We see, dear mistress : and we say, the Gods,
As hitherto they kept him, keep him now.

*Merope.*

O my son !                                                      *str*
I have, I have thee . . . . the years
Fly back, my child ! and thou seem'st

Ne'er to have gone from these eyes,
Never been torn from this breast.

*Æpytus.*

Mother, my heart runs over; but the time
Presses me. chides me, will not let me weep.

*Merope.*

Fearest thou now?

*Æpytus.*

I fear not, but I think on my design.

*Merope.*

At the undried fount of this breast.
A babe, thou smilest again.
Thy brothers play at my feet,
Early-slain innocents! near,
Thy kind-speaking father stands.

*Æpytus.*

Remember, to revenge his death I come!

*Merope.*

Ah . . . revenge!                    *ant.*
That word! it kills me! I see

Once more roll back on my house,
Never to ebb, the accurst
All-flooding ocean of blood.

*Æpytus.*

Mother, sometimes the justice of the Gods
Appoints the way to peace through shedding blood.

*Merope.*

Sorrowful peace !

*Æpytus.*

And yet the only peace to us allow'd.

*Merope.*

From the first-wrought vengeance is born
A long succession of crimes.
Fresh blood flows, calling for blood.
Fathers, sons, grandsons, are all
One death-dealing vengeful train.

*Æpytus.*

Mother, thy fears are idle; for I come
To close an old wound, not to open new
In all else willing to be taught, in this

Instruct me not; I have my lesson clear.—
Arcas, seek out my uncle Laias, now
Conferring in the city with our friends;
Here bring him, ere the king come back from council.
That, how to accomplish what the Gods enjoin,
And the slow-ripening time at last prepares,
We two with thee, my mother, may consult;
For whose help dare I count on, if not thine?

*Merope.*

Approves my brother Laias this intent?

*Æpytus.*

Yes, and alone is with me here to share.

*Merope.*

And what of thine Arcadian mate, who bears
Suspicion from thy grandsire of thy death,
For whom, as I suppose, thou passest here?

*Æpytus.*

Sworn to our plot he is; if false surmise
Fix him the author of my death, I know not.

*Merope.*

Proof, not surmise, shows him in commerce close——

*Æpytus.*

With this Messenian tyrant—that I know.

*Merope.*

And entertain'st thou, child, such dangerous friends?

*Æpytus.*

This commerce for my best behoof he plies.

*Merope.*

That thou may'st read thine enemy's counsel plain?

*Æpytus.*

Too dear his secret wiles have cost our house.

*Merope.*

And of his unsure agent what demands he?

*Æpytus.*

News of my business, pastime, temper, friends.

*Merope.*

His messages, then, point not to thy murder?

*Æpytus.*

Not yet, though such, no doubt, his final aim.

*Merope.*

And what Arcadian helpers bring'st thou here?

*Æpytus.*

Laias alone; no errand mine for crowds.

*Merope.*

On what relying, to crush such a foe?

*Æpytus.*

One sudden stroke, and the Messenians' love.

*Merope.*

O thou long-lost, long seen in dreams alone,
But now seen face to face, my only child!
Why wilt thou fly to lose as soon as found
My new-won treasure, thy belovéd life?
Or how expectest not to lose, who com'st

III G

With such slight means to cope with such a foe?
Thine enemy thou know'st not, nor his strength.
The stroke thou purposest is desperate, rash—
Yet grant that it succeeds—thou hast behind
The stricken king a second enemy
Scarce dangerous less than him, the Dorian lords.
These are not now the savage band who erst
Follow'd thy father from their northern hills,
Mere ruthless and uncounsell'd wolves of war,
Good to obey, without a leader nought.
Their chief hath train'd them, made them like himself,
Sagacious, men of iron, watchful, firm,
Against surprise and sudden panic proof.
Their master fall'n, these will not flinch, but band
To keep their master's power; thou wilt find
Behind his corpse their hedge of serried spears.
But, to match these, thou hast the people's love?
On what a reed, my child, thou leanest there!
Knowest thou not how timorous, how unsure,
How useless an ally a people is
Against the one and certain arm of power?
Thy father perish'd in this people's cause,
Perish'd before their eyes, yet no man stirr'd!
For years, his widow, in their sight I stand,
A never-changing index to revenge—

What help, what vengeance, at their hands have I?—
At least, if thou wilt trust them, try them first.
Against the King himself array the host
Thou countest on to back thee 'gainst his lords;
First rally the Messenians to thy cause,
Give them cohesion, purpose, and resolve,
Marshal them to an army—then advance,
Then try the issue; and not, rushing on
Single and friendless, give to certain death
That dear-beloved, that young, that gracious head.
Be guided, O my son! spurn counsel not!
For know thou this, a violent heart hath been
Fatal to all the race of Heracles.


*The Chorus.*

With sage experience she speaks; and thou,
O Æpytus, weigh well her counsel given.


*Æpytus.*

Ill counsel, in my judgment, gives she here,
Maidens, and reads experience much amiss;
Discrediting the succour which our cause
Might from the people draw, if rightly used;
Advising us a course which would, indeed,

If follow'd, make their succour slack and null.
A people is no army, train'd to fight,
A passive engine, at their general's will ;
And, if so used, proves, as thou say'st, unsure.
A people, like a common man, is dull,
Is lifeless, while its heart remains untouch'd ;
A fool can drive it, and a fly may scare.
When it admires and loves, its heart awakes :
Then irresistibly it lives, it works ;
A people, then, is an ally indeed—
It is ten thousand fiery wills in one.
Now I, if I invite them to run risk
Of life for my advantage, and myself,
Who chiefly profit, run no more than they—
How shall I rouse their love, their ardour so ?
But, if some signal, unassisted stroke,
Dealt at my own sole risk, before their eyes,
Announces me their rightful prince return'd—
The undegenerate blood of Heracles—
The daring claimant of a perilous throne—
How might not such a sight as this revive
Their loyal passion tow'rd my father's house,
Kindle their hearts, make them no more a mob,
A craven mob, but a devouring fire ?
Then might I use them, then, for one who thus

Spares not himself, themselves they will not spare.

Haply, had but one daring soul stood forth

To rally them and lead them to revenge,

When my great father fell, they had replied!

Alas! our foe alone stood forward then.

And thou, my mother, hadst thou made a sign—

Hadst thou, from thy forlorn and captive state

Of widowhood in these polluted halls,

Thy prison-house, raised one imploring cry—

Who knows but that avengers thou hadst found?

But mute thou sat'st, and each Messenian heart

In thy despondency desponded too.

Enough of this!—Though not a finger stir

To succour me in my extremest need;

Though all free spirits in this land were dead,

And only slaves and tyrants left alive;

Yet for me, mother, I had liefer die

On native ground, than drag the tedious hours

Of a protected exile any more.

Hate, duty, interest, passion call one way;

Here stand I now, and the attempt shall be.

*The Chorus.*

Prudence is on the other side; but deeds

Condemn'd by prudence have sometimes gone well.

*Merope.*

Not till the ways of prudence all are tried,
And tried in vain, the turn of rashness comes.
Thou leapest to thy deed, and hast not ask'd
Thy kinsfolk and thy father's friends for aid.


*Æpytus.*

And to what friends should I for aid apply?


*Merope.*

The royal race of Temenus, in Argos——


*Æpytus.*

That house, like ours, intestine murder maims.


*Merope.*

Thy Spartan cousins, Procles and his brother——


*Æpytus.*

Love a won cause, but not a cause to win.


*Merope.*

My father, then, and his Arcadian chiefs——

*Æpytus.*

Mean still to keep aloof from Dorian broil.

*Merope.*

Wait, then, until sufficient help appears.

*Æpytus.*

Orestes in Mycenæ had no more.

*Merope.*

He to fulfil an order raised his hand.

*Æpytus.*

What order more precise had he than I?

*Merope.*

Apollo peal'd it from his Delphian cave.

*Æpytus.*

A mother's murder needed hest divine.

*Merope.*

He had a hest, at least, and thou hast none.

*Æpytus.*

The Gods command not where the heart speaks clear

*Merope.*

Thou wilt destroy, I see, thyself and us.

*Æpytus.*

O suffering ! O calamity ! how ten,
How twentyfold worse are ye, when your blows
Not only wound the sense, but kill the soul,
The noble thought, which is alone the man !
That I, to-day returning, find myself
Orphan'd of both my parents—by his foes
My father, by your strokes my mother slain !
For this is not my mother, who dissuades,
At the dread altar of her husband's tomb,
His son from vengeance on his murderer ;
And not alone dissuades him, but compares
His just revenge to an unnatural deed,
A deed so awful, that the general tongue
Fluent of horrors, falters to relate it—
Of darkness so tremendous, that its author,
Though to his act empower'd, nay, impell'd,
By the oracular sentence of the Gods,

Fled, for years after, o'er the face of earth,
A frenzied wanderer, a God-driven man,
And hardly yet, some say, hath found a grave—
With such a deed as *this* thou matchest mine,
Which Nature sanctions, which the innocent blood
Clamours to find fulfill'd, which good men praise,
And only bad men joy to see undone!
O honour'd father! hide thee in thy grave
Deep as thou canst, for hence no succour comes;
Since from thy faithful subjects what revenge
Canst thou expect, when thus thy widow fails?
Alas! an adamantine strength indeed,
Past expectation, hath thy murderer built;
For this is the true strength of guilty kings,
When they corrupt the souls of those they rule.

### The Chorus.

Zeal makes him most unjust; but, in good time,
Here, as I guess, the noble Laias comes.

### Laias.

Break off, break off your talking, and depart
Each to his post, where the occasion calls;
Lest from the council-chamber presently
The King return, and find you prating here

A time will come for greetings; but to-day
The hour for words is gone, is come for deeds.

### Æpytus.

O princely Laias! to what purpose calls
The occasion, if our chief confederate fails?
My mother stands aloof, and blames our deed.

### Laias.

My royal sister? . . . but, without some cause,
I know, she honours not the dead so ill.

### Merope.

Brother, it seems thy sister must present,
At this first meeting after absence long,
Not welcome, exculpation to her kin;
Yet exculpation needs it, if I seek,
A woman and a mother, to avert
Risk from my new-restored, my only son?—
Sometimes, when he was gone, I wish'd him back,
Risk what he might; now that I have him here,
Now that I feed mine eyes on that young face,
Hear that fresh voice, and clasp that gold-lock'd head,
I shudder, Laias, to commit my child
To murder's dread arena, where I saw

His father and his ill-starr'd brethren fall!
I loathe for him the slippery way of blood;
I ask if bloodless means may gain his end.
In me the fever of revengeful hate,
Passion's first furious longing to imbrue
Our own right hand in the detested blood
Of enemies, and count their dying groans—
If in this feeble bosom such a fire
Did ever burn—is long by time allay'd,
And I would now have Justice strike, not me.
Besides—for from my brother and my son
I hide not even this—the reverence deep,
Remorseful, tow'rd my hostile solitude,
By Polyphontes never fail'd-in once
Through twenty years; his mournful anxious zeal
To efface in me the memory of his crime—
Though it efface not that, yet makes me wish
His death a public, not a personal act,
Treacherously plotted 'twixt my son and me;
To whom this day he came to proffer peace,
Treaty, and to this kingdom for my son
Heirship, with fair intent, as I believe.—
For that he plots thy death, account it false;

> [to ÆPYTUS

Number it with the thousand rumours vain,

Figments of plots, wherewith intriguers fill
The enforcéd leisure of an exile's ear.
Immersed in serious state-craft is the King,
Bent above all to pacify, to rule,
Rigidly, yet in settled calm, this realm;
Not prone, all say, averse to bloodshed now.—
So much is due to truth, even tow'rds our foe.

*[to* LAIAS

Do I, then, give to usurpation grace,
And from his natural rights my son debar?
Not so! let him—and none shall be more prompt
Than I to help—raise his Messenian friends;
Let him fetch succours from Arcadia, gain
His Argive or his Spartan cousins' aid;
Let him do this, do aught but recommence
Murder's uncertain, secret, perilous game—
And I, when to his righteous standard down
Flies Victory wing'd, and Justice raises *then*
Her sword, will be the first to bid it fall.
If, haply, at this moment, such attempt
Promise not fair, let him a little while
Have faith, and trust the future and the Gods.
He may; for never did the Gods allow
Fast permanence to an ill-gotten throne.—
These are but woman's words—yet, Laias, thou

Despise them not! for, brother, thou and I
Were not among the feuds of warrior-chiefs,
Each sovereign for his dear-bought hour, born;
But in the pastoral Arcadia rear'd,
With Cypselus our father, where we saw
The simple patriarchal state of kings,
Where sire to son transmits the unquestion'd crown,
Unhack'd, unsmirch'd, unbloodied, and have learnt
That spotless hands unshaken sceptres hold.
Having learnt this, then, use thy knowledge now.


*The Chorus.*

Which way to lean I know not: bloody strokes
Are never free from doubt, though sometimes due.


*Laias.*

O Merope, the common heart of man
Agrees to deem some deeds so dark in guilt,
That neither gratitude, nor tie of race,
Womanly pity, nor maternal fear,
Nor any pleader else, shall be indulged
To breathe a syllable to bar revenge.
All this, no doubt, thou to thyself hast urged—
Time presses, so that theme forbear I now:

Direct to thy dissuasions I reply.

Blood-founded thrones, thou say'st, are insecure;

Our father's kingdom, because pure, is safe.

True; but what cause to our Arcadia gives

Its privileged immunity from blood,

But that, since first the black and fruitful Earth

In the primeval mountain-forests bore

Pelasgus, our forefather and mankind's,

Legitimately sire to son, with us,

Bequeaths the allegiance of our shepherd-tribes,

More loyal, as our line continues more?—

How can your Heracleidan chiefs inspire

This awe which guards our earth-sprung, lineal kings?

What permanence, what stability like ours,

Whether blood flows or no, can yet invest

The broken order of your Dorian thrones,

Fix'd yesterday, and ten times changed since then?—

Two brothers, and their orphan nephews, strove

For the three conquer'd kingdoms of this isle;

The eldest, mightiest brother, Temenus, took

Argos; a juggle to Cresphontes gave

Messenia; to those helpless Boys, the lot

Worst of the three, the stony Sparta, fell.

August, indeed, was the foundation here!

What follow'd?—His most trusted kinsman slew

Cresphontes in Messenia; Temenus
Perish'd in Argos by his jealous sons;
The Spartan Brothers with their guardian strive.
Can houses thus ill-seated, thus embroil'd,
Thus little founded in their subjects' love,
Practise the indulgent, bloodless policy
Of dynasties long-fix'd, and honour'd long?
No! Vigour and severity must chain
Popular reverence to these recent lines.
Be their first-founded order strict maintain'd—
Their murder'd rulers terribly avenged—
Ruthlessly their rebellious subjects crush'd!
Since policy bids thus, what fouler death
Than thine illustrious husband's to avenge
Shall we select? than Polyphontes, what
More daring and more grand offender find?
Justice, my sister, long demands this blow,
And Wisdom, now thou see'st, demands it too.
To strike it, then, dissuade thy son no more;
For to live disobedient to these two,
Justice and Wisdom, is no life at all.

### The Chorus.

The Gods, O mistress dear! the hard-soul'd man,
Who spared not others, bid not us to spare.

### Merope.

Alas! against my brother, son, and friends,
One, and a woman, how can I prevail?—
O brother, thou hast conquer'd; yet, I fear!
Son! with a doubting heart thy mother yields:
May it turn happier than my doubts portend!

### Laius.

Meantime on thee the task of silence only
Shall be imposed; to us shall be the deed.
Now, not another word, but to our act!
Nephew! thy friends are sounded, and prove true.
Thy father's murderer, in the public place,
Performs, this noon, a solemn sacrifice;
Be with him—choose the moment—strike thy blow!
If prudence counsels thee to go unarm'd,
The sacrificer's axe will serve thy turn.
To me and the Messenians leave the rest,
With the Gods' aid—and, if they give but aid
As our just cause deserves, I do not fear

[ÆPYTUS, LAIAS, *and* ARCAS, *go out.*

### The Chorus.

O Son and Mother,                                    *str.* 1.
Whom the Gods o'ershadow,

In dangerous trial,
With certainty of favour !
As erst they shadow'd
Your race's founders
From irretrievable woe ;
When the seed of Lycaon
Lay forlorn, lay outcast,
Callisto and her Boy.


What deep-grass'd meadow                    *ant.* 1.
At the meeting valleys—
Where clear-flowing Ladon,
Most beautiful of waters,
Receives the river
Whose trout are vocal,
The Aroanian stream—
Without home, without mother,
Hid the babe, hid Arcas,
The nursling of the dells ?


But the sweet-smelling myrtle,                    *str* 2
And the pink-flower'd oleander,
And the green agnus-castus,
To the west-wind's murmur,

III                                        H

Rustled round his cradle ;
And Maia rear'd him.
Then, a boy, he startled,
In the snow-fill'd hollows
Of high Cyllenê,
The white mountain-birds ;
Or surprised, in the glens,
The basking tortoises,
Whose striped shell founded
In the hand of Hermes
The glory of the lyre.

But his mother, Callisto,         *ant.* 2
In her hiding-place of the thickets
Of the lentisk and ilex,
In her rough form, fearing
The hunter on the outlook,
Poor changeling ! trembled.
Or the children, plucking
In the thorn-choked gullies
Wild gooseberries, scared her,
The shy mountain-bear !
Or the shepherds, on slopes
With pale-spiked lavender
And crisp thyme tufted,

Came upon her, stealing
At day-break through the dew.

Once, 'mid those gorges,                    *str.* 3.
Spray-drizzled, lonely,
Unclimb'd of man—
O'er whose cliffs the townsmen
Of crag-perch'd Nonacris
Behold in summer
The slender torrent
Of Styx come dancing,
A wind-blown thread—
By the precipices of Khelmos,
The fleet, desperate hunter,
The youthful Arcas, born of Zeus,
His fleeing mother,
Transform'd Callisto,
Unwitting follow'd—
And raised his spear.

Turning, with piteous,                      *ant.* 3
Distressful longing,
Sad, eager eyes,
Mutely she regarded
Her well-known enemy.

Low moans half utter'd
What speech refused her;
Tears coursed, tears human,
Down those disfigured,
Once human cheeks.
With unutterable foreboding
Her son, heart-stricken, eyed her
The Gods had pity, made them Stars
Stars now they sparkle
In the northern Heaven—
The guard Arcturus,
The guard-watch'd Bear.


So, o'er thee and thy child,                    *epode*
Some God, Merope, now,
In dangerous hour, stretches his hand.
So, like a star, dawns thy son,
Radiant with fortune and joy.

[POLYPHONTES *comes in*

*Polyphontes.*

O Merope, the trouble on thy face
Tells me enough thou know'st the news which all
Messenia speaks! the prince, thy son, is dead.
Not from my lips should consolation fall:

To offer that, I come not; but to urge,
Even after news of this sad death, our league.
Yes, once again I come; I will not take
This morning's angry answer for thy last.
To the Messenian kingdom thou and I
Are the sole claimants left; what cause of strife
Lay in thy son is buried in his grave.
Most honourably I meant, I call the Gods
To witness, offering him return and power;
Yet, had he lived, suspicion, jealousy,
Inevitably had surged up, perhaps,
'Twixt thee and me—suspicion, that I nursed
Some ill design against him; jealousy,
That he enjoy'd but part, being heir to all.
And he himself, with the impetuous heart
Of youth, 'tis like, had never quite forgone
The thought of vengeance on me, never quite
Unclosed his itching fingers from his sword.
But thou, O Merope, though deeply wrong'd,
Though injured past forgiveness, as men deem,
Yet hast been long at school with thoughtful time,
And from that teacher may'st have learn'd, like me,
That all may be endured, and all forgiv'n—
Have learn'd, that we must sacrifice the bent
Of personal feeling to the public weal—

Have learn'd, that there are guilty deeds, which leave
The hand that does them guiltless; in a word,
That kings live for their peoples, not themselves.
This having known, let us a union found
(For the last time I ask, ask earnestly)
Based on pure public welfare; let us be
Not Merope and Polyphontes, foes
Blood-sever'd, but Messenia's King and Queen!
Let us forget ourselves for those we rule!
Speak! I go hence to offer sacrifice
To the Preserver Zeus; let me return
Thanks to him for our amity as well.

*Merope.*

Oh had'st thou, Polyphontes, still but kept
The silence thou hast kept for twenty years!

*Polyphontes.*

Henceforth, if what I urge displease, I may.
But fair proposal merits fair reply.

*Merope.*

And thou shalt have it! Yes, because thou *hast*
For twenty years forborne to interrupt
The solitude of her whom thou hast wrong'd—

That scanty grace shall earn thee this reply.—
First, for our union.   Trust me, 'twixt us two
The brazen-footed Fury ever stalks,
Waving her hundred hands, a torch in each,
Aglow with angry fire, to keep us twain.
Now, for thyself.   Thou com'st with well-cloak'd
    joy,
To announce the ruin of my husband's house,
To sound thy triumph in his widow's ears,
To bid her share thine unendanger'd throne.
To this thou would'st have answer.   Take it: Fly!...
Cut short thy triumph, seeming at its height;
Fling off thy crown, supposed at last secure;
Forsake this ample, proud Messenian realm;
To some small, humble, and unnoted strand,
Some rock more lonely than that Lemnian isle
Where Philoctetes pined, take ship and flee!
Some solitude more inaccessible
Than the ice-bastion'd Caucasian Mount
Chosen a prison for Prometheus, climb!
There in unvoiced oblivion sink thy name,
And bid the sun, thine only visitant,
Divulge not to the far-off world of men
What once-famed wretch he there did espy hid.
There nurse a late remorse, and thank the Gods,

And thank thy bitterest foe, that, having lost
All things but life, thou lose not life as well.

*Polyphontes.*

What mad bewilderment of grief is this?

*Merope.*

*Thou* art bewilder'd; the sane head is mine.

*Polyphontes.*

I pity thee, and wish thee calmer mind.

*Merope.*

Pity thyself; none needs compassion more

*Polyphontes.*

Yet, oh! could'st thou but act as reason bids!

*Merope.*

And in my turn I wish the same for thee.

*Polyphontes.*

All I could do to soothe thee has been tried.

*Merope.*

For that, in this my warning, thou art paid.

*Polyphontes.*

Know'st thou then aught, that thus thou sound'st the
 alarm?

*Merope.*

Thy crime! that were enough to make one fear.

*Polyphontes.*

My deed is of old date, and long atoned.

*Merope.*

Atoned this very day, perhaps, it is.

*Polyphontes.*

My final victory proves the Gods appeased.

*Merope.*

O victor, victor, trip not at the goal!

*Polyphontes.*

Hatred and passionate envy blind thine eyes.

*Merope.*

O Heaven-abandon'd wretch, that envies thee!

*Polyphontes.*

Thou hold'st so cheap, then, the Messenian crown?

*Merope.*

I think on what the future hath in store.

*Polyphontes.*

To-day I reign; the rest I leave to Fate.

*Merope.*

For Fate thou wait'st not long; since, in this hour——

*Polyphontes.*

What? for so far Fate hath not proved my foe—

*Merope.*

Fate seals my lips, and drags to ruin thee

*Polyphontes.*

Enough! enough! I will no longer hear
The ill-boding note which frantic hatred sounds
To affright a fortune which the Gods secure.
Once more my friendship thou rejectest; well!
More for this land's sake grieve I, than mine own.

I chafe not with thee, that thy hate endures,
Nor bend myself too low, to make it yield.
What I have done is done ; by my own deed,
Neither exulting nor ashamed, I stand.
Why should this heart of mine set mighty store
By the construction and report of men ?
Not men's good word hath made me what I am.
Alone I master'd power ; and alone,
Since so thou wilt, I dare maintain it still.

[POLYPHONTES *goes out.*

### *The Chorus.*

Did I then waver                                            *str.* 1.
(O woman's judgment !)
Misled by seeming
Success of crime ?
And ask, if sometimes
The Gods, perhaps, allow'd you,
O lawless daring of the strong,
O self-will recklessly indulged ?

Not time, not lightning,                                    *ant.* 1
Not rain, not thunder,
Efface the endless
Decrees of Heaven—

Make Justice alter,
Revoke, assuage her sentence,
Which dooms dread ends to dreadful deeds,
And violent deaths to violent men.


But the signal example     *str.* 2
Of invariableness of justice
Our glorious founder
Heracles gave us,
Son loved of Zeus his father—for he sinn'd,


And the strand of Eubœa,     *ant* 2
And the promontory of Cenæum,
His painful, solemn
Punishment witness'd,
Beheld his expiation—for he died.


O villages of Œta      *str* 3.
With hedges of the wild rose!
O pastures of the mountain,
Of short grass, beaded with dew,
Between the pine-woods and the cliffs!
O cliffs, left by the eagles,
On that morn, when the smoke-cloud

From the oak-built, fiercely-burning pyre,
Up the precipices of Trachis,
Drove them screaming from their eyries!
A willing, a willing sacrifice on that day
Ye witness'd, ye mountain lawns,
When the shirt-wrapt, poison-blister'd Hero
Ascended, with undaunted heart,
Living, his own funeral-pile,
And stood, shouting for a fiery torch;
And the kind, chance-arrived Wanderer,[1]
The inheritor of the bow,
Coming swiftly through the sad Trachinians,
Put the torch to the pile.
That the flame tower'd on high to the Heaven;
Bearing with it, to Olympus,
To the side of Hebe,
To immortal delight,
The labour-released Hero.

O heritage of Neleus,          *ant.* 3.
Ill-kept by his infirm heirs!
O kingdom of Messenê,
Of rich soil, chosen by craft,
Possess'd in hatred, lost in blood!
O town, high Stenyclaros.

With new walls, which the victors
From the four-town'd, mountain-shadow'd Doris,
For their Heracles-issued princes
Built in strength against the vanquish'd !
Another, another sacrifice on this day
Ye witness, ye new-built towers !
When the white-robed, garland-crowned Monarch
Approaches, with undoubting heart,
Living, his own sacrifice-block,
And stands, shouting for a slaughterous axe ;
And the stern, destiny-brought Stranger,
The inheritor of the realm,
Coming swiftly through the jocund Dorians,
Drives the axe to its goal.
That the blood rushes in streams to the dust :
Bearing with it, to Erinnys,
To the Gods of Hades,
To the dead unavenged,
The fiercely-required Victim.

Knowing he did it, unknowing pays for it.    [*epode.*
Unknowing, unknowing,
Thinking atoned-for
Deeds unatonable,
Thinking appeased

Gods unappeasable,
Lo, the ill-fated one,
Standing for harbour
Right at the harbour-mouth
Strikes with all sail set
Full on the sharp-pointed
Needle of ruin !

[*A* MESSENGER *comes in.*

### Messenger.

O honour'd Queen, O faithful followers
Of your dead master's line, I bring you news
To make the gates of this long-mournful house
Leap, and fly open of themselves for joy !

[*noise and shouting heard*

Hark how the shouting crowds tramp hitherward
With glad acclaim !   Ere they forestall my news,
Accept it :—Polyphontes is no more.

### Merope.

Is my son safe ? that question bounds my care.

### Messenger.

He is, and by the people hail'd for king.

*Merope.*

The rest to me is little ; yet, since that
Must from some mouth be heard, relate it thou


*Messenger.*

Not little, if thou saw'st what love, what zeal,
At thy dead husband's name the people show.
For when this morning in the public square
I took my stand, and saw the unarm'd crowds
Of citizens in holiday attire,
Women and children intermix'd ; and then,
Group'd around Zeus's altar, all in arms,
Serried and grim, the ring of Dorian lords—
I trembled for our prince and his attempt.
Silence and expectation held us all ;
Till presently the King came forth, in robe
Of sacrifice, his guards clearing the way
Before him—at his side, the prince, thy son,
Unarm'd and travel-soil'd, just as he was.
With him conferring the King slowly reach'd
The altar in the middle of the square,
Where, by the sacrificing minister,
The flower-dress'd victim stood—a milk-white bull,

Swaying from side to side his massy head
With short impatient lowings.   There he stopp'd,
And seem'd to muse awhile, then raised his eyes
To heaven, and laid his hand upon the steer,
And cried : *O Zeus, let what blood-guiltiness*
*Yet stains our land be by this blood wash'd out,*
*And grant henceforth to the Messenians peace !*
That moment, while with upturn'd eyes he pray'd,
The prince snatch'd from the sacrificer's hand
The axe, and on the forehead of the King,
Where twines the chaplet, dealt a mighty blow
Which fell'd him to the earth, and o'er him stood,
And shouted : *Since by thee defilement came,*
*What blood so meet as thine to wash it out ?*
*What hand to strike thee meet as mine, the hand*
*Of Æpytus, thy murder'd master's son ?*—
But, gazing at him from the ground, the King . . .
*Is it, then, thou ?* he murmur'd ; and with that,
He bow'd his head, and deeply groan'd, and
        died.
Till then we all seem'd stone, but then a cry
Broke from the Dorian lords ; forward they rush'd
To circle the prince round—when suddenly
Laias in arms sprang to his nephew's side,
Crying : *O ye Messenians, will ye leave*

III                                                    I

*The son to perish as ye left the sire?*
And from that moment I saw nothing clear;
For from all sides a deluge, as it seem'd
Burst o'er the altar and the Dorian lords,
Of holiday-clad citizens transform'd
To armed warriors;—I heard vengeful cries,
I heard the clash of weapons; then I saw
The Dorians lying dead, thy son hail'd king.
And, truly, one who sees, what seem'd so strong,
The power of this tyrant and his lords,
Melt like a passing smoke, a nightly dream,
At one bold word, one enterprising blow—
Might ask, why we endured their yoke so long;
But that we know how every perilous feat
Of daring, easy as it seems when done,
Is easy at no moment but the right.


*The Chorus.*


Thou speakest well; but here, to give our eyes
Authentic proof of what thou tell'st our ears,
The conquerors, with the King's dead body, come.

> [ÆPYTUS, LAIAS, *and* ARCAS *come in with the
> dead body of* POLYPHONTES, *followed by a
> crowd of the* MESSENIANS.

*Laias.*

Sister, from this day forth thou art no more
The widow of a husband unavenged,
The anxious mother of an exiled son.
Thine enemy is slain, thy son is king!
Rejoice with us! and trust me, he who wish'd
Welfare to the Messenian state, and calm,
Could find no way to found them sure as this.

*Æpytus.*

Mother, all these approve me; but if thou
Approve not too, I have but half my joy.

*Merope.*

O Æpytus, my son, behold, behold
This iron man, my enemy and thine,
This politic sovereign, lying at our feet,
With blood-bespatter'd robes, and chaplet shorn!
Inscrutable as ever, see, it keeps
Its sombre aspect of majestic care,
Of solitary thought, unshared resolve,
Even in death, that countenance austere!
So look'd he, when to Stenyclaros first,
A new-made wife, I from Arcadia came,

And found him at my husband's side, his friend,

His kinsman, his right hand in peace and war,

Unsparing in his service of his toil,

His blood—to me, for I confess it, kind;

So look'd he in that dreadful day of death;

So, when he pleaded for our league but now.

What meantest thou, O Polyphontes, what

Desired'st thou, what truly spurr'd thee on?

Was policy of state, the ascendency

Of the Heracleidan conquerors, as thou said'st,

Indeed thy lifelong passion and sole aim?

Or did'st thou but, as cautious schemers use,

Cloak thine ambition with these specious words?

I know not; just, in either case, the stroke

Which laid thee low, for blood requires blood;

But yet, not knowing this, I triumph not

Over thy corpse—triumph not, neither mourn,—

For I find worth in thee, and badness too.

What mood of spirit, therefore, shall we call

The true one of a man—what way of life

His fix'd condition and perpetual walk?

None, since a twofold colour reigns in all.

But thou, my son, study to make prevail

One colour in thy life, the hue of truth:

That justice, that sage order, not alone

Natural vengeance, may maintain thine act,
And make it stand indeed the will of Heaven.
Thy father's passion was this people's case,
This people's anarchy, thy foe's pretence.
As the chiefs rule, my son, the people are.
Unhappy people, where the chiefs themselves
Are, like the mob, vicious and ignorant!
So rule, that even thine enemies may fail
To find in thee a fault whereon to found,
Of tyrannous harshness, or remissness weak—
So rule, that as thy father thou be loved!
So rule, that as his foe thou be obey'd!
Take these, my son, over thine enemy's corpse
Thy mother's prayers! and this prayer last of all:
That even in thy victory thou show,
Mortal, the moderation of a man.

### *Æpytus.*

O mother, my best diligence shall be
In all by thy experience to be ruled
Where my own youth falls short! But, Laias, now,
First work after such victory, let us go
To render to my true Messenians thanks,
To the Gods grateful sacrifice; and then,
Assume the ensigns of my father's power.

*The Chorus.*

Son of Cresphontes, past what perils
Com'st thou, guided safe, to thy home !
What things daring ! what enduring !
And all this by the will of the Gods.

# EMPEDOCLES ON ETNA

## A DRAMATIC POEM

# PERSONS.

Empedocles.

Pausanias, *a Physician.*

Callicles, *a young Harp-player.*

*The Scene of the Poem is on Mount Etna ; at first in the forest region, afterwards on the summit of the mountain.*

# EMPEDOCLES ON ETNA.

## ACT I. SCENE I.

*Morning.    A Pass in the forest region of Etna.*

### CALLICLES.

*(Alone, resting on a rock by the path.)*

THE mules, I think, will not be here this hour;
They feel the cool wet turf under their feet
By the stream-side, after the dusty lanes
In which they have toil'd all night from Catana,
And scarcely will they budge a yard.   O Pan,
How gracious is the mountain at this hour!
A thousand times have I been here alone,
Or with the revellers from the mountain-towns,
But never on so fair a morn;—the sun
Is shining on the brilliant mountain-crests,
And on the highest pines; but farther down,
Here in the valley, is in shade; the sward
Is dark, and on the stream the mist still hangs;

One sees one's footprints crush'd in the wet grass,
One's breath curls in the air; and on these pines
That climb from the stream's edge, the long grey tufts,
Which the goats love, are jewell'd thick with dew.
Here will I stay till the slow litter comes.
I have my harp too—that is well.—Apollo!
What mortal could be sick or sorry here?
I know not in what mind Empedocles,
Whose mules I follow'd, may be coming up,
But if, as most men say, he is half mad
With exile, and with brooding on his wrongs,
Pausanias, his sage friend, who mounts with him,
Could scarce have lighted on a lovelier cure.
The mules must be below, far down.   I hear
Their tinkling bells, mix'd with the song of birds,
Rise faintly to me—now it stops!—Who's here?
Pausanias! and on foot? alone?


*Pausanias.*

                              And thou, then?
I left thee supping with Peisianax,
With thy head full of wine, and thy hair crown'd,
Touching thy harp as the whim came on thee,
And praised and spoil'd by master and by guests

Almost as much as the new dancing-girl.
Why hast thou follow'd us?

### Callicles.

> The night was hot,
> And the feast past its prime; so we slipp'd out,
> Some of us, to the portico to breathe;—
> Peisianax, thou know'st, drinks late;—and then,
> As I was lifting my soil'd garland off,
> I saw the mules and litter in the court,
> And in the litter sate Empedocles;
> Thou, too, wast with him.   Straightway I sped home;
> I saddled my white mule, and all night long
> Through the cool lovely country follow'd you,
> Pass'd you a little since as morning dawn'd,
> And have this hour sate by the torrent here,
> Till the slow mules should climb in sight again.
> And now?

### Pausanias.

> And now, back to the town with speed!
> Crouch in the wood first, till the mules have pass'd;
> They do but halt, they will be here anon.
> Thou must be viewless to Empedocles;

Save mine, he must not meet a human eye.

One of his moods is on him that thou know'st;

I think, thou wouldst not vex him.

### Callicles.

No—and yet

I would fain stay, and help thee tend him.   Once

He knew me well, and would oft notice me;

And still, I know not how, he draws me to him,

And I could watch him with his proud sad face,

His flowing locks and gold-encircled brow

And kingly gait, for ever; such a spell

In his severe looks, such a majesty

As drew of old the people after him,

In Agrigentum and Olympia,

When his star reign'd, before his banishment,

Is potent still on me in his decline.

But oh! Pausanias, he is changed of late;

There is a settled trouble in his air

Admits no momentary brightening now,

And when he comes among his friends at feasts,

'Tis as an orphan among prosperous boys.

Thou know'st of old he loved this harp of mine,

When first he sojourn'd with Peisianax;

He is now always moody, and I fear him;

But I would serve him, soothe him, if I could,
Dared one but try.

Pausanias.

        Thou wast a kind child ever !
He loves thee, but he must not see thee now.
Thou hast indeed a rare touch on thy harp,
He loves that in thee, too ;—there was a time
(But that is pass'd), he would have paid thy strain
With music to have drawn the stars from heaven.
He hath his harp and laurel with him still,
But he has laid the use of music by,
And all which might relax his settled gloom.
Yet thou may'st try thy playing, if thou wilt—
But thou must keep unseen ; follow us on,
But at a distance ! in these solitudes,
In this clear mountain-air, a voice will rise,
Though from afar, distinctly ; it may soothe him.
Play when we halt, and, when the evening comes
And I must leave him (for his pleasure is
To be left musing these soft nights alone
In the high unfrequented mountain-spots),
Then watch him, for he ranges swift and far,
Sometimes to Etna's top, and to the cone ;
But hide thee in the rocks a great way down,

And try thy noblest strains, my Callicles,
With the sweet night to help thy harmony!
Thou wilt earn my thanks sure, and perhaps his.


### Callicles.

More than a day and night, Pausanias,
Of this fair summer-weather, on these hills,
Would I bestow to help Empedocles.
That needs no thanks; one is far better here
Than in the broiling city in these heats.
But tell me, how hast thou persuaded him
In this his present fierce, man-hating mood,
To bring thee out with him alone on Etna?


### Pausanias.

Thou hast heard all men speaking of Pantheia,
The woman who at Agrigentum lay
Thirty long days in a cold trance of death,
And whom Empedocles call'd back to life.
Thou art too young to note it, but his power
Swells with the swelling evil of this time,
And holds men mute to see where it will rise.
He could stay swift diseases in old days,
Chain madmen by the music of his lyre,

Cleanse to sweet airs the breath of poisonous streams,
And in the mountain-chinks inter the winds.
This he could do of old; but now, since all
Clouds and grows daily worse in Sicily,
Since broils tear us in twain, since this new swarm
Of sophists has got empire in our schools
Where he was paramount, since he is banish'd
And lives a lonely man in triple gloom—
He grasps the very reins of life and death.
I ask'd him of Pantheia yesterday,
When we were gather'd with Peisianax,
And he made answer, I should come at night
On Etna here, and be alone with him,
And he would tell me, as his old, tried friend,
Who still was faithful, what might profit me;
That is, the secret of this miracle.

### Callicles.

Bah! Thou a doctor! Thou art superstitious.
Simple Pausanias, 'twas no miracle!
Pantheia, for I know her kinsmen well,
Was subject to these trances from a girl.
Empedocles would say so, did he deign;
But he still lets the people, whom he scorns,
Gape and cry *wizard* at him, if they list.

But thou, thou art no company for him!
Thou art as cross, as sour'd as himself!
Thou hast some wrong from thine own citizens,
And then thy friend is banish'd, and on that,
Straightway thou fallest to arraign the times,
As if the sky was impious•not to fall.
The sophists are no enemies of his;
I hear, Gorgias, their chief, speaks nobly of him,
As of his gifted master, and once friend.
He is too scornful, too high-wrought, too bitter.
'Tis not the times, 'tis not the sophists vex him;
There is some root of suffering in himself,
Some secret and unfollow'd vein of woe,
Which makes the time look black and sad to him.
Pester him not in this his sombre mood
With questionings about an idle tale,
But lead him through the lovely mountain-paths,
And keep his mind from preying on itself,
And talk to him of things at hand and common,
Not miracles! thou art a learned man,
But credulous of fables as a girl.


*Pausanias.*

And thou, a boy whose tongue outruns his knowledge,

And on whose lightness blame is thrown away.
Enough of this! I see the litter wind
Up by the torrent-side, under the pines.
I must rejoin Empedocles.   Do thou
Crouch in the brushwood till the mules have pass'd ;
Then play thy kind part well.   Farewell till night !

## SCENE II.

*Noon.    A Glen on the highest skirts of the woody region*
*of Etna.*

EMPEDOCLES.   PAUSANIAS.

*Pausanias.*

The noon is hot.   When we have cross'd the stream,
We shall have left the woody tract, and come
Upon the open shoulder of the hill.
See how the giant spires of yellow bloom
Of the sun-loving gentian, in the heat,
Are shining on those naked slopes like flame !
Let us rest here ; and now, Empedocles,
Pantheia's history !

[*A harp-note below is heard*

*Empedocles.*

                    Hark ! what sound was that
Rose from below ?  If it were possible,
And we were not so far from human haunt,
I should have said that some one touch'd a harp
Hark ! there again !

*Pausanias.*

'Tis the boy Callicles,
The sweetest harp-player in Catana.
He is for ever coming on these hills,
In summer, to all country-festivals,
With a gay revelling band ; he breaks from them
Sometimes, and wanders far among the glens.
But heed him not, he will not mount to us ;
I spoke with him this morning.   Once more, therefore,
Instruct me of Pantheia's story, Master,
As I have pray'd thee.

*Empedocles.*

That ? and to what end ?

*Pausanias.*

It is enough that all men speak of it.
But I will also say, that when the Gods
Visit us as they do with sign and plague,
To know those spells of thine which stay their hand
Were to live free from terror.

*Empedocles.*

Spells ? Mistrust them !
Mind is the spell which governs earth and heaven.

Man has a mind with which to plan his safety ;
Know that, and help thyself !

### Pausanias.

But thine own words ?
" The wit and counsel of man was never clear,
Troubles confound the little wit he has."
Mind is a light which the Gods mock us with,
To lead those false who trust it.

[*The harp sounds again.*

### Empedocles.

Hist ! once more !
Listen, Pausanias !—Ay, 'tis Callicles ;
I know these notes among a thousand.   Hark !

### Callicles.

(*Sings unseen, from below.*)

The track winds down to the clear stream,
To cross the sparkling shallows ; there
The cattle love to gather, on their way
To the high mountain-pastures, and to stay,
Till the rough cow-herds drive them past,
Knee-deep in the cool ford ; for 'tis the last

Of all the woody, high, well-water'd dells
On Etna ; and the beam
Of noon is broken there by chestnut-boughs
Down its steep verdant sides ; the air
Is freshen'd by the leaping stream, which throws
Eternal showers of spray on the moss'd roots
Of trees, and veins of turf, and long dark shoots
Of ivy-plants, and fragrant hanging bells
Of hyacinths, and on late anemonies,
That muffle its wet banks ; but glade,
And stream, and sward, and chestnut-trees,
End here ; Etna beyond, in the broad glare
Of the hot noon, without a shade,
Slope behind slope, up to the peak, lies bare ;
The peak, round which the white clouds play.

In such a glen, on such a day,
On Pelion, on the grassy ground,
Chiron, the aged Centaur lay,
The young Achilles standing by.
The Centaur taught him to explore
The mountains ; where the glens are dry
And the tired Centaurs come to rest,
And where the soaking springs abound
And the straight ashes grow for spears,

And where the hill-goats come to feed,
And the sea-eagles build their nest.
He show'd him Phthia far away,
And said : O boy, I taught this lore
To Peleus, in long distant years !
He told him of the Gods, the stars,
The tides ;—and then of mortal wars,
And of the life which heroes lead
Before they reach the Elysian place
And rest in the immortal mead ;
And all the wisdom of his race.


*The music below ceases, and* EMPEDOCLES *speaks,
accompanying himself in a solemn manner on
his harp.*


The out-spread world to span
A cord the Gods first slung,
And then the soul of man
There, like a mirror, hung,
And bade the winds through space impel the gusty
toy.


Hither and thither spins
The wind-borne, mirroring soul,

A thousand glimpses wins,
And never sees a whole;
Looks once, and drives elsewhere, and leaves its last
employ.


The Gods laugh in their sleeve
To watch man doubt and fear,
Who knows not what to believe
Since he sees nothing clear,
And dares stamp nothing false where he finds nothing
sure.


Is this, Pausanias, so?
And can our souls not strive,
But with the winds must go,
And hurry where they drive?
Is fate indeed so strong, man's strength indeed so
poor?


I will not judge. That man,
Howbeit, I judge as lost,
Whose mind allows a plan,
Which would degrade it most;
And he treats doubt the best who tries to see least ill.

Be not, then, fear's blind slave !
Thou art my friend ; to thee,
All knowledge that I have,
All skill I wield, are free.
Ask not the latest news of the last miracle,

Ask not what days and nights
In trance Pantheia lay,
But ask how thou such sights
May'st see without dismay ;
Ask what most helps when known, thou son of
Anchitus !

What ? hate, and awe, and shame
Fill thee to see our time ;
Thou feelest thy soul's frame
Shaken and out of chime ?
What ? life and chance go hard with thee too, as
with us ;

Thy citizens, 'tis said,
Envy thee and oppress,
Thy goodness no men aid,
All strive to make it less ;
Tyranny, pride, and lust, fill Sicily's abodes,

Heaven is with earth at strife,
Signs make thy soul afraid,
The dead return to life,
Rivers are dried, winds stay'd;
Scarce can one think in calm, so threatening are
the Gods;


And we feel, day and night,
The burden of ourselves—
Well, then, the wiser wight
In his own bosom delves,
And asks what ails him so, and gets what cure he can.


The sophist sneers : Fool, take
Thy pleasure, right or wrong.
The pious wail : Forsake
A world these sophists throng.
Be neither saint nor sophist-led, but be a man !


These hundred doctors try
To preach thee to their school.
We have the truth ! they cry;
And yet their oracle,
Trumpet it as they will, is but the same as thine.

Once read thy own breast right,
And thou hast done with fears ;
Man gets no other light,
Search he a thousand years.
Sink in thyself ! there ask what ails thee, at that shrine !


What makes thee struggle and rave ?
Why are men ill at ease ?—
'Tis that the lot they have
Fails their own will to please ;
For man would make no murmuring, were his will
          obey'd.


And why is it, that still
Man with his lot thus fights ?—
'Tis that he makes this *will*
The measure of his *rights*,
And believes Nature outraged if his will 's gainsaid


Couldst thou, Pausanias, learn
How deep a fault is this ;
Couldst thou but once discern
Thou hast no *right* to bliss,
No title from the Gods to welfare and repose ;

Then thou wouldst look less mazed
Whene'er of bliss debarr'd,
Nor think the Gods were crazed
When thy own lot went hard.
But we are all the same—the fools of our own woes!


For, from the first faint morn
Of life, the thirst for bliss
Deep in man's heart is born;
And, sceptic as he is,
He fails not to judge clear if this be quench'd or no


Nor is the thirst to blame.
Man errs not that he deems
His welfare his true aim,
He errs because he dreams
The world does but exist that welfare to bestow.


We mortals are no kings
For each of whom to sway
A new-made world up-springs,
Meant merely for his play;
No, we are strangers here; the world is from of old.

In vain our pent wills fret,
And would the world subdue.
Limits we did not set
Condition all we do;
Born into life we are, and life must be our mould.


Born into life!—man grows
Forth from his parents' stem,
And blends their bloods, as those
Of theirs are blent in them;
So each new man strikes root into a far fore-time.


Born into life!—we bring
A bias with us here,
And, when here, each new thing
Affects us we come near;
To tunes we did not call our being must keep chime.


Born into life!—in vain,
Opinions, those or these,
Unalter'd to retain
The obstinate mind decrees;
Experience, like a sea, soaks all-effacing in.

Born into life !—who lists
May what is false hold dear,
And for himself make mists
Through which to see less clear :
The world is what it is, for all our dust and din.

Born into life !—'tis we,
And not the world, are new ;
Our cry for bliss, our plea,
Others have urged it too—
Our wants have all been felt, our errors made before.

No eye could be too sound
To observe a world so vast,
No patience too profound
To sort what's here amass'd ;
How man may here best live no care too great to
explore.

But we—as some rude guest
Would change, where'er he roam,
The manners there profess'd
To those he brings from home—
We mark not the world's course, but would have *it*
take *ours*.

The world's course proves the terms
On which man wins content;
Reason the proof confirms—
We spurn it, and invent
A false course for the world, and for ourselves, false
powers.

Riches we wish to get,
Yet remain spendthrifts still;
We would have health, and yet
Still use our bodies ill;
Bafflers of our own prayers, from youth to life's last
scenes.

We would have inward peace,
Yet will not look within;
We would have misery cease,
Yet will not cease from sin;
We want all pleasant ends, but will use no harsh
means;

We do not what we ought,
What we ought not, we do,
And lean upon the thought
That chance will bring us through;
But our own acts, for good or ill, are mightier powers.

Yet, even when man forsakes
All sin,—is just, is pure,
Abandons all which makes
His welfare insecure,—
Other existences there are, that clash with ours.


Like us, the lightning-fires
Love to have scope and play;
The stream, like us, desires
An unimpeded way;
Like us, the Libyan wind delights to roam at large.


Streams will not curb their pride
The just man not to entomb,
Nor lightnings go aside
To give his virtues room;
Nor is that wind less rough which blows a good
man's barge.


Nature, with equal mind,
Sees all her sons at play;
Sees man control the wind,
The wind sweep man away;
Allows the proudly-riding and the foundering bark.

And, lastly, though of ours
No weakness spoil our lot,
Though the non-human powers
Of Nature harm us not,
The ill deeds of other men make often *our* life dark


What were the wise man's plan?—
Through this sharp, toil-set life,
To work as best he can,
And win what's won by strife.—
But we an easier way to cheat our pains have found.


Scratch'd by a fall, with moans
As children of weak age
Lend life to the dumb stones
Whereon to vent their rage,
And bend their little fists, and rate the senseless
            ground ;


So, loath to suffer mute,
We, peopling the void air,
Make Gods to whom to impute
The ills we ought to bear ;
With God and Fate to rail at, suffering easily.

Yet grant—as sense long miss'd
Things that are now perceived,
And much may still exist
Which is not yet believed—
Grant that the world were full of Gods we cannot see;

All things the world which fill
Of but one stuff are spun,
That we who rail are still,
With what we rail at, one;
One with the o'erlabour'd Power that through the
breadth and length

Of earth, and air, and sea,
In men, and plants, and stones,
Hath toil perpetually,
And travails, pants, and moans;
Fain would do all things well, but sometimes fails in
strength.

And patiently exact
This universal God
Alike to any act
Proceeds at any nod,
And quietly declaims the cursings of himself.

This is not what man hates,
Yet he can curse but this.
Harsh Gods and hostile Fates
Are dreams ! this only *is*—
Is everywhere ; sustains the wise, the foolish elf.


Nor only, in the intent
To attach blame elsewhere,
Do we at will invent
Stern Powers who make their care
To embitter human life, malignant Deities ;


But, next, we would reverse
The scheme ourselves have spun,
And what we made to curse
We now would lean upon,
And feign kind Gods who perfect what man vainly
tries.


Look, the world tempts our eye,
And we would know it all !
We map the starry sky,
We mine this earthen ball,
We measure the sea-tides, we number the sea-sands ;

We scrutinise the dates
Of long-past human things,
The bounds of effaced states,
The lines of deceased kings;
We search out dead men's words, and works of dead
men's hands;

We shut our eyes, and muse
How our own minds are made,
What springs of thought they use,
How righten'd, how betray'd—
And spend our wit to name what most employ
unnamed.

But still, as we proceed
The mass swells more and more
Of volumes yet to read,
Of secrets yet to explore.
Our hair grows grey, our eyes are dimm'd, our heat
is tamed;

We rest our faculties,
And thus address the Gods:
"True science if there is,
It stays in your abodes!
Man's measures cannot mete the immeasurable All.

" You only can take in
The world's immense design.
Our desperate search was sin,
Which henceforth we resign,
Sure only that your mind sees all things which befal."


Fools !   That in man's brief term
He cannot all things view,
Affords no ground to affirm
That there are Gods who do ;
Nor does being weary prove that he has where tc
          rest.


Again.—Our youthful blood
Claims rapture as its right ;
The world, a rolling flood
Of newness and delight,
Draws in the enamour'd gazer to its shining breast ;


Pleasure, to our hot grasp,
Gives flowers after flowers ;
With passionate warmth we clasp
Hand after hand in ours ;
Now do we soon perceive how fast our youth is spent.

At once our eyes grow clear !
We see, in blank dismay,
Year posting after year,
Sense after sense decay ;
Our shivering heart is mined by secret discontent ;


Yet still, in spite of truth,
In spite of hopes entomb'd,
That longing of our youth
Burns ever unconsumed,
Still hungrier for delight as delights grow more rare.


We pause ; we hush our heart,
And thus address the Gods :
" The world hath fail'd to impart
The joy our youth forebodes,
Fail'd to fill up the void which in our breasts we bear.


" Changeful till now, we still
Look'd on to something new ;
Let us, with changeless will,
Henceforth look on to you,
To find with you the joy we in vain here require ! "

Fools!   That so often here
Happiness mock'd our prayer,
I think, might make us fear
A like event elsewhere;
Make us, not fly to dreams, but moderate desire.

And yet, for those who know
Themselves, who wisely take
Their way through life, and bow
To what they cannot break,
Why should I say that life need yield but *moderate*
        bliss?

Shall we, with temper spoil'd,
Health sapp'd by living ill,
And judgment all embroil'd
By sadness and self-will,
Shall *we* judge what for man is not true bliss or is?

Is it so small a thing
To have enjoy'd the sun,
To have lived light in the spring,
To have loved, to have thought, to have done;
To have advanced true friends, and beat down baffling
        foes—

That we must feign a bliss
Of doubtful future date,
And, while we dream on this,
Lose all our present state,
And relegate to worlds yet distant our repose?


Not much, I know, you prize
What pleasures may be had,
Who look on life with eyes
Estranged, like mine, and sad;
And yet the village-churl feels the truth more than you,


Who's loath to leave this life
Which to him little yields—
His hard-task'd sunburnt wife,
His often-labour'd fields,
The boors with whom he talk'd, the country-spots he
knew.


But thou, because thou hear'st
Men scoff at Heaven and Fate,
Because the Gods thou fear'st
Fail to make blest thy state,
Tremblest, and wilt not dare to trust the joys there are!

I say: Fear not! Life still
Leaves human effort scope.
But, since life teems with ill,
Nurse no extravagant hope;
Because thou must not dream, thou need'st not then
despair!

*A long pause. At the end of it the notes of a harp
below are again heard, and* CALLICLES *sings:*—

Far, far from here,
The Adriatic breaks in a warm bay
Among the green Illyrian hills; and there
The sunshine in the happy glens is fair,
And by the sea, and in the brakes.
The grass is cool, the sea-side air
Buoyant and fresh, the mountain flowers
More virginal and sweet than ours.
And there, they say, two bright and aged snakes,
Who once were Cadmus and Harmonia,
Bask in the glens or on the warm sea-shore,
In breathless quiet, after all their ills;
Nor do they see their country, nor the place
Where the Sphinx lived among the frowning hills,
Nor the unhappy palace of their race,
Nor Thebes, nor the Ismenus, any more.

There those two live, far in the Illyrian brakes!
They had stay'd long enough to see,
In Thebes, the billow of calamity
Over their own dear children roll'd,
Curse upon curse, pang upon pang,
For years, they sitting helpless in their home,
A grey old man and woman; yet of old
The Gods had to their marriage come,
And at the banquet all the Muses sang.

Therefore they did not end their days
In sight of blood; but were rapt, far away,
To where the west-wind plays,
And murmurs of the Adriatic come
To those untrodden mountain-lawns; and there
Placed safely in changed forms, the pair
Wholly forget their first sad life, and home,
And all that Theban woe, and stray
For ever through the glens, placid and dumb.

*Empedocles.*

That was my harp-player again!—where is he?
Down by the stream?

*Pausanias.*

Yes, Master, in the wood.

*Empedocles.*

He ever loved the Theban story well!
But the day wears.   Go now, Pausanias,
For I must be alone.   Leave me one mule;
Take down with thee the rest to Catana.
And for young Callicles, thank him from me;
Tell him, I never fail'd to love his lyre—
But he must follow me no more to-night.

*Pausanias.*

Thou wilt return to-morrow to the city?

*Empedocles.*

Either to-morrow or some other day,
In the sure revolutions of the world,
Good friend, I shall revisit Catana.
I have seen many cities in my time,
Till mine eyes ache with the long spectacle,
And I shall doubtless see them all again;
Thou know'st me for a wanderer from of old.
Meanwhile, stay me not now.   Farewell, Pausanias!

*He departs on his way up the mountain.*

*Pausanias (alone).*

I dare not urge him further—he must go ;
But he is strangely wrought !—I will speed back
And bring Peisianax to him from the city ;
His counsel could once soothe him.   But, Apollo !
How his brow lighten'd as the music rose !
Callicles must wait here, and play to him ;
I saw him through the chestnuts far below,
Just since, down at the stream.—Ho ! Callicles !

*He descends, calling.*

## ACT II.

*Evening.　The Summit of Etna.*

### EMPEDOCLES.

Alone !—
On this charr'd, blacken'd, melancholy waste,
Crown'd by the awful peak, Etna's great mouth.
Round which the sullen vapour rolls—alone !
Pausanias is far hence, and that is well,
For I must henceforth speak no more with man
He hath his lesson too, and that debt's paid ;
And the good, learned, friendly, quiet man,
May bravelier front his life, and in himself
Find henceforth energy and heart.　But I—
The weary man, the banish'd citizen,
Whose banishment is not his greatest ill,
Whose weariness no energy can reach,
And for whose hurt courage is not the cure—
What should I do with life and living more ?

No, thou art come too late, Empedocles!
And the world hath the day, and must break thee,
Not thou the world.   With men thou canst not live,
Their thoughts, their ways, their wishes, are not thine;
And being lonely thou art miserable,
For something has impair'd thy spirit's strength,
And dried its self-sufficing fount of joy.
Thou canst not live with men nor with thyself—
O sage! O sage!—Take then the one way left;
And turn thee to the elements, thy friends,
Thy well-tried friends, thy willing ministers,
And say: Ye helpers, hear Empedocles,
Who asks this final service at your hands!
Before the sophist-brood hath overlaid
The last spark of man's consciousness with words—
Ere quite the being of man, ere quite the world
Be disarray'd of their divinity—
Before the soul lose all her solemn joys,
And awe be dead, and hope impossible,
And the soul's deep eternal night come on—
Receive me, hide me, quench me, take me home!

> *He advances to the edge of the crater.  Smoke*
> *and fire break forth with a loud noise, and*
> CALLICLES *is heard below singing :—*

The lyre's voice is lovely everywhere ;
In the court of Gods, in the city of men,
And in the lonely rock-strewn mountain-glen,
In the still mountain air.

Only to Typho it sounds hatefully ;
To Typho only, the rebel o'erthrown,
Through whose heart Etna drives her roots of stone
To imbed them in the sea.

Wherefore dost thou groan so loud ?
Wherefore do thy nostrils flash,
Through the dark night, suddenly,
Typho, such red jets of flame ?—
Is thy tortured heart still proud ?
Is thy fire-scathed arm still rash ?
Still alert thy stone-crush'd frame ?
Doth thy fierce soul still deplore
Thine ancient rout by the Cilician hills,
And that curst treachery on the Mount of Gore ? [2]
Do thy bloodshot eyes still weep

The fight which crown'd thine ills,
Thy last mischance on this Sicilian deep?
Hast thou sworn, in thy sad lair,
Where erst the strong sea-currents suck'd thee
      down,
Never to cease to writhe, and try to rest,
Letting the sea-stream wander through thy hair
That thy groans, like thunder prest,
Begin to roll, and almost drown
The sweet notes whose lulling spell
Gods and the race of mortals love so well,
When through thy caves thou hearest music swell?

But an awful pleasure bland
Spreading o'er the Thunderer's face,
When the sound climbs near his seat,
The Olympian council sees;
As he lets his lax right hand,
Which the lightnings doth embrace,
Sink upon his mighty knees.
And the eagle, at the beck
Of the appeasing, gracious harmony,
Droops all his sheeny, brown, deep-feather'd neck,
Nestling nearer to Jove's feet;
While o'er his sovran eye

The curtains of the blue films slowly meet,
And the white Olympus-peaks
Rosily brighten, and the soothed Gods smile
At one another from their golden chairs,
And no one round the charmed circle speaks.
Only the loved Hebe bears
The cup about, whose draughts beguile
Pain and care, with a dark store
Of fresh-pull'd violets wreathed and nodding o'er .
And her flush'd feet glow on the marble floor.

*Empedocles.*

He fables, yet speaks truth !
The brave, impetuous heart yields everywhere
To the subtle, contriving head ;
Great qualities are trodden down,
And littleness united
Is become invincible.


These rumblings are not Typho's groans, I know !
These angry smoke-bursts
Are not the passionate breath
Of the mountain-crush'd, tortured, intractable
        Titan king—

But over all the world
What suffering is there not seen
Of plainness oppress'd by cunning,
As the well-counsell'd Zeus oppress'd
That self-helping son of earth!
What anguish of greatness,
Rail'd and hunted from the world,
Because its simplicity rebukes
This envious, miserable age!

I am weary of it.
—Lie there, ye ensigns
Of my unloved preëminence
In an age like this!
Among a people of children,
Who throng'd me in their cities,
Who worshipp'd me in their houses,
And ask'd, not wisdom,
But drugs to charm with,
But spells to mutter—
All the fool's-armoury of magic!—Lie there,
My golden circlet,
My purple robe!

*Callicles (from below).*

As the sky-brightening south-wind clears the
      day,
And makes the mass'd clouds roll,
The music of the lyre blows away
The clouds which wrap the soul.


Oh! that Fate had let me see
That triumph of the sweet persuasive lyre,
That famous, final victory,
When jealous Pan with Marsyas did conspire;


When, from far Parnassus' side,
Young Apollo, all the pride
Of the Phrygian flutes to tame,
To the Phrygian highlands came;
Where the long green reed-beds sway
In the rippled waters grey
Of that solitary lake
Where Mæander's springs are born;
Whence the ridged pine-wooded roots
Of Messogis westward break,
Mounting westward, high and higher.

There was held the famous strife ;
There the Phrygian brought his flutes,
And Apollo brought his lyre ;
And, when now the westering sun
Touch'd the hills, the strife was done,
And the attentive Muses said :
"Marsyas, thou art vanquished !"
Then Apollo's minister
Hang'd upon a branching fir
Marsyas, that unhappy Faun,
And began to whet his knife.
But the Mænads, who were there,
Left their friend, and with robes flowing
In the wind, and loose dark hair
O'er their polish'd bosoms blowing,
Each her ribbon'd tambourine
Flinging on the mountain-sod,
With a lovely frighten'd mien
Came about the youthful God.
But he turn'd his beauteous face
Haughtily another way,
From the grassy sun-warm'd place
Where in proud repose he lay,
With one arm over his head,
Watching how the whetting sped.

But aloof, on the lake-strand,
Did the young Olympus stand,
Weeping at his master's end;
For the Faun had been his friend.
For he taught him how to sing,
And he taught him flute-playing.
Many a morning had they gone
To the glimmering mountain-lakes,
And had torn up by the roots
The tall crested water-reeds
With long plumes and soft brown
        seeds,
And had carved them into flutes,
Sitting on a tabled stone
Where the shoreward ripple breaks.
And he taught him how to please
The red-snooded Phrygian girls,
Whom the summer evening sees
Flashing in the dance's whirls
Underneath the starlit trees
In the mountain-villages.
Therefore now Olympus stands,
At his master's piteous cries
Pressing fast with both his hands
His white garment to his eyes,

Not to see Apollo's scorn ;—
Ah, poor Faun, poor Faun ! ah, poor Faun !


*Empedocles.*

And lie thou there,
My laurel bough !
Scornful Apollo's ensign, lie thou there !
Though thou hast been my shade in the world's heat—
Though I have loved thee, lived in honouring thee—
Yet lie thou there,
My laurel bough !


I am weary of thee.
I am weary of the solitude
Where he who bears thee must abide—
Of the rocks of Parnassus,
Of the gorge of Delphi,
Of the moonlit peaks, and the caves.
Thou guardest them, Apollo !
Over the grave of the slain Pytho,
Though young, intolerably severe !
Thou keepest aloof the profane,
But the solitude oppresses thy votary !
The jars of men reach him not in thy valley—

But can life reach him ?
Thou fencest him from the multitude—
Who will fence him from himself ?
He hears nothing but the cry of the torrents,
And the beating of his own heart.
The air is thin, the veins swell,
The temples tighten and throb there—
Air ! air !


Take thy bough, set me free from my solitude ;
I have been enough alone !


Where shall thy votary fly then ? back to men ?—
But they will gladly welcome him once more,
And help him to unbend his too tense thought,
And rid him of the presence of himself,
And keep their friendly chatter at his ear,
And haunt him, till the absence from himself,
That other torment, grow unbearable ;
And he will fly to solitude again,
And he will find its air too keen for him,
And so change back ; and many thousand times
Be miserably bandied to and fro
Like a sea-wave, betwixt the world and thee,

Thou young, implacable God! and only death
Can cut his oscillations short, and so
Bring him to poise.   There is no other way.

And yet what days were those, Parmenides!
When we were young, when we could number friends
In all the Italian cities like ourselves,
When with elated hearts we join'd your train,
Ye Sun-born Virgins! on the road of truth.[3]
Then we could still enjoy, then neither thought
Nor outward things were closed and dead to us;
But we received the shock of mighty thoughts
On simple minds with a pure natural joy;
And if the sacred load oppress'd our brain,
We had the power to feel the pressure eased,
The brow unbound, the thoughts flow free again,
In the delightful commerce of the world.
We had not lost our balance then, nor grown
Thought's slaves, and dead to every natural joy.
The smallest thing could give us pleasure then—
The sports of the country-people,
A flute-note from the woods,
Sunset over the sea;
Seed-time and harvest,
The reapers in the corn,

The vinedresser in his vineyard,
The village-girl at her wheel.


Fulness of life and power of feeling, ye
Are for the happy, for the souls at ease,
Who dwell on a firm basis of content!
But he, who has outlived his prosperous days—
But he, whose youth fell on a different world
From that on which his exiled age is thrown—
Whose mind was fed on other food, was train'd
By other rules than are in vogue to-day—
Whose habit of thought is fix'd, who will not change,
But, in a world he loves not, must subsist
In ceaseless opposition, be the guard
Of his own breast, fetter'd to what he guards,
That the world win no mastery over him—
Who has no friend, no fellow left, not one;
Who has no minute's breathing space allow'd
To nurse his dwindling faculty of joy——
Joy and the outward world must die to him,
As they are dead to me.

*A long pause, during which* EMPEDOCLES *remains motionless, plunged in thought. The night deepens. He moves forward and gazes round him, and proceeds:—*

And you, ye stars,
Who slowly begin to marshal,
As of old, in the fields of heaven,
Your distant, melancholy lines!
Have you, too, survived yourselves?
Are you, too, what I fear to become?
You, too, once lived;
You too moved joyfully
Among august companions,
In an older world, peopled by Gods,
In a mightier order,
The radiant, rejoicing, intelligent Sons of Heaven
But now, ye kindle
Your lonely, cold-shining lights,
Unwilling lingerers
In the heavenly wilderness,
For a younger, ignoble world;
And renew, by necessity,
Night after night your courses,
In echoing, unnear'd silence,

Above a race you know not—
Uncaring and undelighted,
Without friend and without home ;
Weary like us, though not
Weary with our weariness.


No, no, ye stars ! there is no death with you,
No languor, no decay ! languor and death,
They are with me, not you ! ye are alive—
Ye, and the pure dark ether where ye ride
Brilliant above me !   And thou, fiery world,
That sapp'st the vitals of this terrible mount
Upon whose charr'd and quaking crust I stand—
Thou, too, brimmest with life !—the sea of
    cloud,
That heaves its white and billowy vapours up
To moat this isle of ashes from the world,
Lives ; and that other fainter sea, far down,
O'er whose lit floor a road of moonbeams leads
To Etna's Liparëan sister-fires
And the long dusky line of Italy—
That mild and luminous floor of waters lives,
With held-in joy swelling its heart ; I only,
Whose spring of hope is dried, whose spirit has
    fail'd,

I, who have not, like these, in solitude
Maintain'd courage and force, and in myself
Nursed an immortal vigour—I alone
Am dead to life and joy, therefore I read
In all things my own deadness.

*A long silence. He continues :—*

Oh, that I could glow like this mountain !
Oh, that my heart bounded with the swell of the
  sea !
Oh, that my soul were full of light as the stars !
Oh, that it brooded over the world like the air !


But no, this heart will glow no more ; thou art
A living man no more, Empedocles !
Nothing but a devouring flame of thought—
But a naked, eternally restless mind !

*After a pause :—*

To the elements it came from
Everything will return—
Our bodies to earth,
Our blood to water,
Heat to fire,
Breath to air.

They were well born, they will be well entomb'd—
But mind? . . .

And we might gladly share the fruitful stir
Down in our mother earth's miraculous womb;
Well would it be
With what roll'd of us in the stormy main;
We might have joy, blent with the all-bathing air,
Or with the nimble, radiant life of fire.

But mind, but thought—
If these have been the master part of us—
Where will *they* find their parent element?
What will receive *them*, who will call *them* home?
But we shall still be in them, and they in us,
And we shall be the strangers of the world,
And they will be our lords, as they are now;
And keep us prisoners of our consciousness,
And never let us clasp and feel the All
But through their forms, and modes, and stifling
          veils.
And we shall be unsatisfied as now;
And we shall feel the agony of thirst,
The ineffable longing for the life of life
Baffled for ever; and still thought and mind

Will hurry us with them on their homeless march,

Over the unallied unopening earth,

Over the unrecognising sea; while air

Will blow us fiercely back to sea and earth,

And fire repel us from its living waves.

And then we shall unwillingly return

Back to this meadow of calamity,

This uncongenial place, this human life;

And in our individual human state

Go through the sad probation all again,

To see if we will poise our life at last,

To see if we will now at last be true

To our own only true, deep-buried selves,

Being one with which we are one with the whole
world;

Or whether we will once more fall away

Into some bondage of the flesh or mind,

Some slough of sense, or some fantastic maze

Forged by the imperious lonely thinking-power.

And each succeeding age in which we are born

Will have more peril for us than the last;

Will goad our senses with a sharper spur,

Will fret our minds to an intenser play,

Will make ourselves harder to be discern'd.

And we shall struggle awhile, gasp and rebel—
And we shall fly for refuge to past times,
Their soul of unworn youth, their breath of
          greatness ;
And the reality will pluck us back,
Knead us in its hot hand, and change our nature.
And we shall feel our powers of effort flag,
And rally them for one last fight—and fail ;
And we shall sink in the impossible strife,
And be astray for ever.


                    Slave of sense
I have in no wise been ;—but slave of thought ? . .
And who can say : I have been always free,
Lived ever in the light of my own soul ?—
I cannot ; I have lived in wrath and gloom,
Fierce, disputatious, ever at war with man,
Far from my own soul, far from warmth and light
But I have not grown easy in these bonds—
But I have not denied what bonds these were.
Yea, I take myself to witness,
That I have loved no darkness,
Sophisticated no truth,
Nursed no delusion,
Allow'd no fear !

And therefore, O ye elements! I know—
Ye know it too—it hath been granted me
Not to die wholly, not to be all enslaved.
I feel it in this hour.   The numbing cloud
Mounts off my soul; I feel it, I breathe free.


Is it but for a moment?
—Ah, boil up, ye vapours!
Leap and roar, thou sea of fire!
My soul glows to meet you.
Ere it flag, ere the mists
Of despondency and gloom
Rush over it again,
Receive me, save me!

[*He plunges into the crater*

*Callicles*

(*from below*).

Through the black, rushing smoke-bursts,
Thick breaks the red flame;
All Etna heaves fiercely
Her forest-clothed frame.

Not here, O Apollo !
Are haunts meet for thee.
But, where Helicon breaks down
In cliff to the sea,

Where the moon-silver'd inlets
Send far their light voice
Up the still vale of Thisbe,
O speed, and rejoice !

On the sward at the cliff-top
Lie strewn the white flocks,
On the cliff-side the pigeons
Roost deep in the rocks.

In the moonlight the shepherds,
Soft lull'd by the rills,
Lie wrapt in their blankets
Asleep on the hills.

—What forms are these coming
So white through the gloom ?
What garments out-glistening
The gold-flower'd broom ?

What sweet-breathing presence
Out-perfumes the thyme?
What voices enrapture
The night's balmy prime?—


'Tis Apollo comes leading
His choir, the Nine.
—The leader is fairest,
But all are divine.


They are lost in the hollows!
They stream up again!
What seeks on this mountain
The glorified train?—


They bathe on this mountain,
In the spring by their road;
Then on to Olympus,
Their endless abode.


—Whose praise do they mention?
Of what is it told?—
What will be for ever;
What was from of old.

III                                             N

First hymn they the Father
Of all things ; and then,
The rest of immortals,
The action of men.

The day in his hotness,
The strife with the palm ;
The night in her silence,
The stars in their calm

# LATER POEMS

# WESTMINSTER ABBEY

## July 25, 1881.

*(The Day of Burial, in the Abbey, of* Arthur Penrhyn
Stanley, *Dean of Westminster.)*

WHAT! for a term so scant
　　Our shining visitant
Cheer'd us, and now is pass'd into the night?
　　Couldst thou no better keep, O Abbey old,
　　The boon thy dedication-sign foretold,[4]
The presence of that gracious inmate, light?—
　　A child of light appear'd;
Hither he came, late-born and long-desired,
　　And to men's hearts this ancient place endear'd;
What, is the happy glow so soon expired?


　　—Rough was the winter eve;
　　Their craft the fishers leave,

And down over the Thames the darkness drew.
   One still lags last, and turns, and eyes the Pile
   Huge in the gloom, across in Thorney Isle,
King Sebert's work, the wondrous Minster new.
    —'Tis Lambeth now, where then
They moor'd their boats among the bulrush stems;
   And that new Minster in the matted fen
The world-famed Abbey by the westering Thames.


   His mates are gone, and he
   For mist can scarcely see
A strange wayfarer coming to his side—
   Who bade him loose his boat, and fix his oar,
   And row him straightway to the further shore,
And wait while he did there a space abide.
   The fisher awed obeys,
That voice had note so clear of sweet command;
   Through pouring tide he pulls, and drizzling
   haze,
And sets his freight ashore on Thorney strand.


   The Minster's outlined mass
   Rose dim from the morass,
And thitherward the stranger took his way.

Lo, on a sudden all the Pile is bright!
Nave, choir and transept glorified with light,
While tongues of fire on coign and carving play!
And heavenly odours fair
Come streaming with the floods of glory in,
And carols float along the happy air,
As if the reign of joy did now begin.

Then all again is dark;
And by the fisher's bark
The unknown passenger returning stands.
*O Saxon fisher! thou hast had with thee*
*The fisher from the Lake of Galilee—*
So saith he, blessing him with outspread hands;
Then fades, but speaks the while:
*At dawn thou to King Sebert shalt relate*
*How his St. Peter's Church in Thorney Isle*
*Peter, his friend, with light did consecrate.*

Twelve hundred years and more
Along the holy floor
Pageants have pass'd, and tombs of mighty kings
Efface the humbler graves of Sebert's line,
And, as years sped, the minster-aisles divine
Grew used to the approach of Glory's wings.

Arts came, and arms, and law,
And majesty, and sacred form and fear;
Only that primal guest the fisher saw,
Light, only light, was slow to reappear.


The Saviour's happy light,
Wherein at first was dight
His boon of life and immortality,
In desert ice of subtleties was spent
Or drown'd in mists of childish wonderment,
Fond fancies here, there false philosophy!
And harsh the temper grew
Of men with mind thus darken'd and astray;
And scarce the boon of life could struggle
through,
For want of light which should the boon convey.


Yet in this latter time
The promise of the prime
Seem'd to come true at last, O Abbey old!
It seem'd, a child of light did bring the dower
Foreshown thee in thy consecration-hour,
And in thy courts his shining freight unroll'd:
Bright wits, and instincts sure,

And goodness warm, and truth without alloy,
  And temper sweet, and love of all things pure,
And joy in light, and power to spread the joy.


  And on that countenance bright
  Shone oft so high a light,
That to my mind there came how, long ago,
  Lay on the hearth, amid a fiery ring,
  The charm'd babe of the Eleusinian king—[5]
His nurse, the Mighty Mother, will'd it so.
  Warm in her breast, by day,
He slumber'd, and ambrosia balm'd the child ;
  But all night long amid the flames he lay,
Upon the hearth, and play'd with them, and smiled.


  But once, at midnight deep,
  His mother woke from sleep,
And saw her babe amidst the fire, and scream'd.
  A sigh the Goddess gave, and with a frown
  Pluck'd from the fire the child, and laid him down ;
Then raised her face, and glory round her stream'd.
  The mourning-stole no more
Mantled her form, no more her head was bow'd ;
  But raiment of celestial sheen she wore,
And beauty fill'd her, and she spake aloud :—

"O ignorant race of man!
Achieve your good who can,
If your own hands the good begun undo?
Had human cry not marr'd the work divine,
Immortal had I made this boy of mine;
But now his head to death again is due
And I have now no power
Unto this pious household to repay
Their kindness shown me in my wandering
hour."
—She spake, and from the portal pass'd away.


The Boy his nurse forgot,
And bore a mortal lot.
Long since, his name is heard on earth no more.
In some chance battle on Cithæron-side
The nursling of the Mighty Mother died,
And went where all his fathers went before.
—On thee too, in thy day
Of childhood, Arthur! did some check have
power,
That, radiant though thou wert, thou couldst
but stay,
Bringer of heavenly light, a human hour?

Therefore our happy guest
Knew care, and knew unrest,
And weakness warn'd him, and he fear'd
decline.
And in the grave he laid a cherish'd wife,
And men ignoble harass'd him with strife,
And deadly airs his strength did undermine.
Then from his Abbey fades
The sound beloved of his victorious breath;
And light's fair nursling stupor first invades,
And next the crowning impotence of death.

But hush! This mournful strain,
Which would of death complain,
The oracle forbade, not ill-inspired.—
That Pair, whose head did plan, whose hands did
forge
The Temple in the pure Parnassian gorge,[6]
Finish'd their work, and then a meed required.
"Seven days," the God replied,
"Live happy, then expect your perfect meed!"
Quiet in sleep, the seventh night, they
died.
Death, death was judged the boon supreme indeed.

And truly he who here
Hath run his bright career,
And served men nobly, and acceptance found,
And borne to light and right his witness high,
What could he better wish than then to die,
And wait the issue, sleeping underground?
Why should he pray to range
Down the long age of truth that ripens slow;
And break his heart with all the baffling change,
And all the tedious tossing to and fro?


For this and that way swings
The flux of mortal things,
Though moving inly to one far-set goal.—
What had our Arthur gain'd, to stop and see,
After light's term, a term of cecity,
A Church once large and then grown strait in soul?
To live, and see arise,
Alternating with wisdom's too short reign,
Folly revived, re-furbish'd sophistries,
And pullulating rites externe and vain?


Ay me!   'Tis deaf, that ear
Which joy'd my voice to hear;

Yet would I not disturb thee from thy tomb,
　　Thus sleeping in thine Abbey's friendly shade,
　　And the rough waves of life for ever laid!
I would not break thy rest, nor change thy doom.
　　　　Even as my father, thou—
Even as that loved, that well-recorded friend—
　　Hast thy commission done; ye both may now
Wait for the leaven to work, the let to end.


　　　And thou, O Abbey grey!
　　　Predestined to the ray
By this dear guest over thy precinct shed—
　　Fear not but that thy light once more shall burn,
　　Once more thine immemorial gleam return,
Though sunk be now this bright, this gracious head!
　　　Let but the light appear
And thy transfigured walls be touch'd with flame—
　　Our Arthur will again be present here,
Again from lip to lip will pass his name.

# GEIST'S GRAVE.

FOUR years!—and didst thou stay above
The ground, which hides thee now, but four?
And all that life, and all that love,
Were crowded, Geist! into no more?

Only four years those winning ways,
Which make me for thy presence yearn,
Call'd us to pet thee or to praise,
Dear little friend! at every turn?

That loving heart, that patient soul,
Had they indeed no longer span,
To run their course, and reach their goal,
And read their homily to man?

That liquid, melancholy eye,
From whose pathetic, soul-fed springs
Seem'd surging the Virgilian cry,*
The sense of tears in mortal things—

* *Sunt lacrimæ rerum !*

That steadfast, mournful strain, consoled
By spirits gloriously gay,
And temper of heroic mould—
What, was four years their whole short day?

Yes, only four!—and not the course
Of all the centuries yet to come,
And not the infinite resource
Of Nature, with her countless sum

Of figures, with her fulness vast
Of new creation evermore,
Can ever quite repeat the past,
Or just thy little self restore.

Stern law of every mortal lot!
Which man, proud man, finds hard to bear,
And builds himself I know not what
Of second life I know not where.

But thou, when struck thine hour to go,
On us, who stood despondent by,
A meek last glance of love didst throw,
And humbly lay thee down to die.

Yet would we keep thee in our heart—
Would fix our favourite on the scene,
Nor let thee utterly depart
And be as if thou ne'er hadst been.


And so there rise these lines of verse
On lips that rarely form them now ;
While to each other we rehearse :
*Such ways, such arts, such looks hadst thou !*


We stroke thy broad brown paws again,
We bid thee to thy vacant chair,
We greet thee by the window-pane,
We hear thy scuffle on the stair.


We see the flaps of thy large ears
Quick raised to ask which way we go ;
Crossing the frozen lake, appears
Thy small black figure on the snow !


Nor to us only art thou dear
Who mourn thee in thine English home
Thou hast thine absent master's tear,
Dropt by the far Australian foam

Thy memory lasts both here and there,
And thou shalt live as long as we.
And after that—thou dost not care !
In us was all the world to thee.

Yet, fondly zealous for thy fame,
Even to a date beyond our own
We strive to carry down thy name,
By mounded turf, and graven stone.

We lay thee, close within our reach,
Here, where the grass is smooth and warm,
Between the holly and the beech,
Where oft we watch'd thy couchant form,

Asleep, yet lending half an ear
To travellers on the Portsmouth road ;—
There build we thee, O guardian dear,
Mark'd with a stone, thy last abode !

Then some, who through this garden pass,
When we too, like thyself, are clay,
Shall see thy grave upon the grass,
And stop before the stone, and say :

III                                        O

*People who lived here long ago*
*Did by this stone, it seems, intend*
*To name for future times to know*
*The dachs-hound, Geist, their little friend.*

## POOR MATTHIAS.

POOR MATTHIAS!—Found him lying
Fall'n beneath his perch and dying?
Found him stiff, you say, though warm—
All convulsed his little form?
Poor canary! many a year
Well he knew his mistress dear;
Now in vain you call his name,
Vainly raise his rigid frame,
Vainly warm him in your breast,
Vainly kiss his golden crest,
Smooth his ruffled plumage fine,
Touch his trembling beak with wine.
One more gasp—it is the end!
Dead and mute our tiny friend!
—Songster thou of many a year,
Now thy mistress brings thee here,

Says, it fits that I rehearse,
Tribute due to thee, a verse,
Meed for daily song of yore
Silent now for evermore.


Poor Matthias! Wouldst thou have
More than pity? claim'st a stave?
—Friends more near us than a bird
We dismiss'd without a word.
Rover, with the good brown head,
Great Atossa, they are dead;
Dead, and neither prose nor rhyme
Tells the praises of their prime.
Thou didst know them old and grey,
Know them in their sad decay.
Thou hast seen Atossa sage
Sit for hours beside thy cage;
Thou wouldst chirp, thou foolish bird,
Flutter, chirp—she never stirr'd!
What were now these toys to her?
Down she sank amid her fur;
Eyed thee with a soul resign'd—
And thou deemedst cats were kind!
—Cruel, but composed and bland,
Dumb, inscrutable and grand,

So Tiberius might have sat,
Had Tiberius been a cat.


Rover died—Atossa too.
Less than they to us are you!
Nearer human were their powers,
Closer knit their life with ours.
Hands had stroked them, which are cold,
Now for years, in churchyard mould;
Comrades of our past were they,
Of that unreturning day.
Changed and aging, they and we
Dwelt, it seem'd, in sympathy.
Alway from their presence broke
Somewhat which remembrance woke
Of the loved, the lost, the young—
Yet they died, and died unsung


Geist came next, our little friend;
Geist had verse to mourn his end.
Yes, but that enforcement strong
Which compell'd for Geist a song—
All that gay courageous cheer,
All that human pathos dear;

Soul-fed eyes with suffering worn,
Pain heroically borne,
Faithful love in depth divine—
Poor Matthias, were they thine?


Max and Kaiser we to-day
Greet upon the lawn at play;
Max a dachshound without blot—
Kaiser should be, but is not.
Max, with shining yellow coat,
Prinking ears and dewlap throat—
Kaiser, with his collie face,
Penitent for want of race.
—Which may be the first to die,
Vain to augur, they or I!
But, as age comes on, I know,
Poet's fire gets faint and low;
If so be that travel they
First the inevitable way,
Much I doubt if they shall have
Dirge from me to crown their grave.


Yet, poor bird, thy tiny corse
Moves me, somehow, to remorse;

Something haunts my conscience, brings
Sad, compunctious visitings.
Other favourites, dwelling here,
Open lived to us, and near ;
Well we knew when they were glad,
Plain we saw if they were sad,
Joy'd with them when they were gay,
Soothed them in their last decay ;
Sympathy could feel and show
Both in weal of theirs and woe.

Birds, companions more unknown,
Live beside us, but alone ;
Finding not, do all they can,
Passage from their souls to man.
Kindness we bestow, and praise,
Laud their plumage, greet their lays ;
Still, beneath their feather'd breast,
Stirs a history unexpress'd.
Wishes there, and feelings strong,
Incommunicably throng ;
What they want, we cannot guess,
Fail to track their deep distress—
Dull look on when death is nigh,
Note no change, and let them die.

Poor Matthias! couldst thou speak,
What a tale of thy last week!
Every morning did we pay
Stupid salutations gay,
Suited well to health, but how
Mocking, how incongruous now!
Cake we offer'd, sugar, seed,
Never doubtful of thy need;
Praised, perhaps, thy courteous eye,
Praised thy golden livery.
Gravely thou the while, poor dear!
Sat'st upon thy perch to hear,
Fixing with a mute regard
Us, thy human keepers hard,
Troubling, with our chatter vain,
Ebb of life, and mortal pain—
Us, unable to divine
Our companion's dying sign,
Or o'erpass the severing sea
Set betwixt ourselves and thee,
Till the sand thy feathers smirch
Fallen dying off thy perch!

Was it, as the Grecian sings,
Birds were born the first of things,

Before the sun, before the wind,
Before the gods, before mankind,
Airy, ante-mundane throng—
Witness their unworldly song !
Proof they give, too, primal powers,
Of a prescience more than ours—
Teach us, while they come and go,
When to sail, and when to sow.
Cuckoo calling from the hill,
Swallow skimming by the mill,
Swallows trooping in the sedge,
Starlings swirling from the hedge,
Mark the seasons, map our year,
As they show and disappear.
But, with all this travail sage
Brought from that anterior age,
Goes an unreversed decree
Whereby strange are they and we ,
Making want of theirs, and plan,
Indiscernible by man.

No, away with tales like these
Stol'n from Aristophanes ! [7]
Does it, if we miss your mind,
Prove us so remote in kind ?

Birds! we but repeat on you
What amongst ourselves we do.
Somewhat more or somewhat less,
'Tis the same unskilfulness.
What you feel, escapes our ken—
Know we more our fellow men?
Human suffering at our side,
Ah, like yours is undescried!
Human longings, human fears,
Miss our eyes and miss our ears.
Little helping, wounding much,
Dull of heart, and hard of touch,
Brother man's despairing sign
Who may trust us to divine?
Who assure us, sundering powers
Stand not 'twixt his soul and ours?

Poor Matthias! See, thy end
What a lesson doth it lend!
For that lesson thou shalt have,
Dead canary bird, a stave!
Telling how, one stormy day,
Stress of gale and showers of spray
Drove my daughter small and me
Inland from the rocks and sea.

Driv'n inshore, we follow down
Ancient streets of Hastings town—
Slowly thread them—when behold,
French canary-merchant old
Shepherding his flock of gold
In a low dim-lighted pen
Scann'd of tramps and fishermen!
There a bird, high-coloured, fat,
Proud of port, though something squat—
Pursy, play'd-out Philistine—
Dazzled Nelly's youthful eyne
But, far in, obscure, there stirr'd
On his perch a sprightlier bird,
Courteous-eyed, erect and slim;
And I whisper'd: "Fix on *him!*"
Home we brought him, young and fair,
Songs to trill in Surrey air.
Here Matthias sang his fill,
Saw the cedars of Pains Hill;
Here he pour'd his little soul,
Heard the murmur of the Mole.
Eight in number now the years
He hath pleased our eyes and ears;
Other favourites he hath known
Go, and now himself is gone.

—Fare thee well, companion dear !
Fare for ever well, nor fear,
Tiny though thou art, to stray
Down the uncompanion'd way !
We without thee, little friend,
Many years have not to spend ;
What are left, will hardly be
Better than we spent with thee.

# KAISER DEAD

APRIL 6, 1887.

WHAT, Kaiser dead? The heavy news
Post-haste to Cobham calls the Muse,
From where in Farringford she brews
    The ode sublime,
Or with Pen bryn's bold bard pursues
    A rival rhyme.

Kai's bracelet tail, Kai's busy feet,
Were known to all the village-street.
"What, poor Kai dead?" say all I meet;
    "A loss indeed!"
O for the croon pathetic, sweet,
    Of Robin's reed![8]

Six years ago I brought him down,
A baby dog, from London town;
Round his small throat of black and brown
    A ribbon blue,
And vouch'd by glorious renown
    A dachshound true.

His mother, most majestic dame,
Of blood-unmix'd, from Potsdam came;
And Kaiser's race we deem'd the same—
          No lineage higher.
And so he bore the imperial name.
          But ah, his sire!


Soon, soon the days conviction bring.
The collie hair, the collie swing,
The tail's indomitable ring,
          The eye's unrest—
The case was clear; a mongrel thing
          Kai stood confest.


But all those virtues, which commend
The humbler sort who serve and tend,
Were thine in store, thou faithful friend.
          What sense, what cheer!
To us, declining tow'rds our end,
          A mate how dear!


For Max, thy brother-dog, began
To flag, and feel his narrowing span.
And cold, besides, his blue blood ran,
          Since, 'gainst the classes,

He heard, of late, the Grand Old Man
　　　Incite the masses.

Yes, Max and we grew slow and sad;
But Kai, a tireless shepherd-lad,
Teeming with plans, alert, and glad
　　　In work or play,
Like sunshine went and came, and bade
　　　Live out the day!

Still, still I see the figure smart—
Trophy in mouth, agog to start,
Then, home return'd, once more depart;
　　　Or prest together
Against thy mistress, loving heart,
　　　In winter weather.

I see the tail, like bracelet twirl'd,
In moments of disgrace uncurl'd,
Then at a pardoning word re-furl'd,
　　　A conquering sign;
Crying, "Come on, and range the world,
　　　And never pine."

Thine eye was bright, thy coat it shone;
Thou hadst thine errands, off and on;

In joy thy last morn flew; anon,
   A fit! All's over;
And thou art gone where Geist hath gone,
   And Toss, and Rover.


Poor Max, with downcast, reverent head,
Regards his brother's form outspread;
Full well Max knows the friend is dead
   Whose cordial talk,
And jokes in doggish language said,
   Beguiled his walk.


And Glory, stretch'd at Burwood gate,
Thy passing by doth vainly wait;
And jealous Jock, thy only hate,
   The chiel from Skye,
Lets from his shaggy Highland pate
   Thy memory die.


Well, fetch his graven collar fine,
And rub the steel, and make it shine,
And leave it round thy neck to twine,
   Kai, in thy grave.
There of thy master keep that sign,
   And this plain stave.

# NOTES.

# NOTES.

### NOTE 1, PAGE 109.

*And the kind, chance-arrived Wanderer.*

POIAS, the father of Philoctetes. Passing near, he was attracted by the concourse round the pyre, and at the entreaty of Hercules set fire to it, receiving the bow and arrows of the hero as his reward.

### NOTE 2, PAGE 158.

*And that curst treachery on the Mount of Gore.*

Mount Hæmus, so called, said the legend, from Typho's blood spilt on it in his last battle with Zeus, when the giant's strength failed, owing to the Destinies having a short time before given treacherously to him, for his refreshment, perishable fruits. See APOLLODORUS, *Bibliotheca*, book i, chap. vi.

### NOTE 3, PAGE 167.

*Ye Sun-born Virgins! on the road of truth.*

See the Fragments of Parmenides :

. . . . . . κοῦραι δ' ὁδὸν ἡγεμόνευσον
ἡλιάδες κοῦραι, προλιποῦσαι δώματο. νυκτός
εἰς φάος . . . . . . .

*Couldst thou no better keep, O Abbey old,*
*The boon thy dedication-sign foretold.*

"Ailred of Rievauix, and several other writers, assert that Sebert, king of the East Saxons and nephew of Ethelbert, founded the Abbey of Westminster very early in the seventh century.

"Sulcardus, who lived in the time of William the Conqueror, gives a minute account of the miracle supposed to have been worked at the consecration of the Abbey.

"The church had been prepared against the next day for dedication. On the night preceding, St. Peter appeared on the opposite side of the water to a fisherman, desiring to be conveyed to the farther shore. Having left the boat, St. Peter ordered the fisherman to wait, promising him a reward on his return. An innumerable host from heaven accompanied the apostle, singing choral hymns, while everything was illuminated with a supernatural light. The dedication having been completed, St. Peter returned to the fisherman, quieted his alarm at what had passed, and announced himself as the apostle. He directed the fisherman to go as soon as it was day to the authorities, to state what he had seen and heard, and to inform them that, in corroboration of his testimony, they would find the marks of consecration on the walls of the church. In obedience to the apostle's direction, the fisherman waited on Mellitus, bishop of London, who, going to the church, found not only marks of the chrism, but of the tapers with which the church had been illuminated. Mellitus, therefore, desisted from proceeding to a new consecration, and contented himself with the celebration of the mass."—DUGDALE, *Monasticon Angli-canum* (edition of 1817), vol. i, pp. 265, 266. See also MONTA-LEMBERT, *Les Moines d'Occident*, vol. iii, pp. 428-432.

### NOTE 5, PAGE 185.

*The charm'd babe of the Eleusinian king.*

Demophoön, son of Celeus, king of Eleusis. See, in the *Homeric Hymns*, the *Hymn to Demeter*, 184-298.

### NOTE 6, PAGE 187.

*That Pair, whose head did plan, whose hands did forge*
*The Temple in the pure Parnassian gorge.*

Agamedes and Trophonius, the builders of the temple of Apollo at Delphi. See Plutarch, *Consolatio ad Apollonium*, c. 14.

### NOTE 7, PAGE 201.

*Stol'n from Aristophanes.*

See *The Birds* of Aristophanes, 465-485.

### NOTE 8, PAGE 205.

*Of Robin's reed.*

"Come, join the melancholious croon
    O' Robin's reed."—BURNS, *Poor Mailie's Elegy*

*Printed in Great Britain by* R. & R. CLARK, LIMITED, *Edinburgh.*

DATE DUE